$\mathcal{N}$OVELTY CAKES

ℕOVELTY CAKES

ROSEMARY WADEY

NOTE

1. All spoon measurements are level. Spoon measures can be bought in both imperial and metric sizes to give accurate measurement of small quantities.

2. All eggs are size 2 or 3 unless otherwise stated.

3. All sugar is granulated unless otherwise stated.

4. Preparation times given are an average calculated during recipe testing. However, most of the cakes in this book need time to cool, set and dry and the total hours given for preparation may have been spread over several days.

5. Metric and imperial measurements have been calculated separately. Use one set of measurements only as they are not exact equivalents.

6. Cooking times may vary slightly depending on the individual oven. Cakes should be placed in the centre of an oven unless otherwise specified.

7. Always preheat the oven to the specified temperature.

8. If using a fan-assisted oven, follow the manufacturer's instructions for guidance on temperature adjustments.

9. Symbols have been used to indicate the degree of skill required to make the cakes:
Relatively simple; novice cake decorators could try these.
More adventurous; making these cakes requires some patience and a steady hand.
These are complicated to make, needing time, plenty of patience and some cake decorating experience.

First published in Great Britain in 1988.
This edition published in 1996 by Hamlyn
imprint of Reed Consumer Books Limited
Michelin House, 81 Fulham Road, London SW3 6RB
and Auckland, Melbourne, Singapore and Toronto

© 1988 Reed International Books Limited

ISBN 0 600 58950 1

A CIP catalogue record for this book is available from The British Library.

Produced by Mandarin Offset
Printed in Hong Kong

CONTENTS

CAKES FOR CHILDREN

Imaginatively based on a wide range of the favourite things of childhood, these cakes will appeal to boys and girls of all ages. There is a bright red train or a cart of building blocks to delight little ones and a satisfyingly 'grown-up' electronic keyboard and a popular television character for older children.

Clockwise from top left: Wigwam (see page 32), Coco the Clown (see page 16), Teddy Bears' Picnic (see page 24)

TARQUIN'S TRAIN 🐾

4-egg Quick mix cake (see pages 128-9),
    any flavour
1.25 kg (2½ lb) Fondant moulding paste
    (see page 137)

Butter cream:
175 g (6 oz) butter or soft margarine
300-350 g (10–12 oz) icing sugar, sifted
few drops vanilla essence
approx 2 tablespoons milk

liquid or paste food colourings – orange,
    red, brown and green
225 g (8 oz) apricot jam, sieved
2–3 milk chocolate flake bars
1–2 tubes coloured chocolate buttons
cellophane paper or cling film
approx 2 metres very narrow green ribbon

Preparation time: about 5 hours, plus
cooking and setting
Cooking time: about 45 minutes
Oven: 160°C, 325°F, Gas Mark 3

1. Grease and line a rectangular tin 28 × 11
× 4 cm (11 × 7 × 1½ inches) with greased
greaseproof or non-stick silicone paper
and thoroughly grease and base line a well
washed and dried 425 g (15 oz) empty food
can.
2. Make up the cake mixture and half fill
the food can. Spread the remainder evenly
in the rectangular tin.
3. Cook both in a preheated oven allowing
approx 45 minutes for the large cake and
similar for the can until well risen and firm
to the touch. If the can is cooked below the
cake it will take about 15 minutes longer
than if cooked beside it. Cool the cakes
slightly and then turn out carefully on to a
wire tray.
4. Leave the cakes for at least 12 hours to
'set' then cut the rectangular cake in half
crossways and then lengthways. Cut one
of the small rectangles in half to give two

pieces approx 9 × 6 cm (3½ × 2½ inches).
Scoop the centre out of another piece leaving a rim of about 2 cm (¾ inch) all round.
5. Make up the Butter cream (see page
137) and use a little to stick the two larger
rectangles together for the cab; and the
two smaller rectangles, one on top of the
other for the tender.
6. Colour the Fondant moulding paste a
mid-orange to red. Roll out a piece and
trim to 13 × 23 cm (4½ × 9 inches). Brush
with jam, and wrap around the cylinder
cake. Cut out a circle to fit the end and
attach.
7. Next roll out a piece of fondant and cut
out a piece to fit all round the cab (approx
30 × 12.5 cm/12 × 5 inches) and a square
of approx 7.5 cm (3 inches) to fit the top.
Brush with jam and position.
8. Stand the front of the train on a board of
approx 46 × 25 cm (18 × 10 inches). Stick
the cab to the back of the engine and the
board with more Butter cream, wedging
together, if necessary.
9. Roll out more fondant and cover the
tender by cutting a piece of approx 28 ×
7.5 cm (11 × 3 inches), brush with jam and
wrap around the sides; and then cut out a
rectangle of approx 7.5 × 6 cm (3 × 2½
inches) to fit the top.
10. Roll out more fondant, cut a piece
about 11 × 12.5 cm (4½ × 5 inches), lay
over the top of the truck, moulding it so it
fits into the scooped-out piece. Then cut a
strip to go around the side of approx 40 ×
4.5 cm (16 × 1¾ inches) and attach.
11. Roll a cylindrical funnel from the
orange fondant about 4 × 2.5 cm (1½ × 1
inch) and a rounded 'button' about 2.5 cm
(1 inch) in diameter. Attach these to the
engine as in the picture with Butter cream.
12. Attach the tender and truck behind the
train with Butter cream. (You could couple
each together with a small hook and ring
made of fondant.)

13. Add brown liquid food colouring to the
remaining orange fondant to turn it a mid-
brown colour. Roll a little out thinly and
cut out four ovals approx 2.5 × 1.5 cm (1
× ½ inch); two windows of 5 × 2.5 cm (2
× 1 inch) and a back window of 5 × 2.5
cm (2 × 1 inch).
14. Attach two ovals to the front of the
engine, two to the front of the cab, one
window each side of the cab and the large
window to the back of the cab.
15. Roll out the remaining icing 5 mm (¼
inch) thick and cut out 10 circles of 4 cm
(1½ inches) for wheels. Attach to the train
with Butter cream, two to each side of the
engine, one each side of the tender and
two each side of the truck.
16. Colour the remaining Butter cream to a
pretty green to make a good contrast to the
rest of the colourings. Put most of it into a
piping bag fitted with a small star nozzle
and use it to outline in shells all around the
front of the engine, all round the cab, up
the sides and around the top and along the
base. Then pipe two lines from the cab to
the front of the engine just each side of the
funnel and, if liked, a row around the top
of the funnel.
17. Change the Butter cream to a piping
bag fitted with a No. 2 writing nozzle and
first pipe two small decorations on the
front of the engine and one on each side of
the engine between the wheels.
18. On each wheel mark 8 spokes in Butter
cream and a row of small touching dots all
round the edge of each wheel. Leave to
set.
19. Finally, cut the chocolate flakes into
'logs' of approx 4 cm (1½ inches) and pile
these up on the tender.
20. Tie up 5 or 6 small bundles of Smarties
or other small sweets in cellophane paper
or cling film and tie with narrow green ribbon with bows. Use these to fill the truck.

BUILDING BRICKS

4-egg Quick mix cake, any flavour (see pages 128-9) or 4-egg Madeira cake mix (see pages 130-1)

1.5 kg (3¼ lb) Fondant moulding paste (see page 137)

liquid or paste food colourings – yellow, blue, green and red or orange

6 tablespoons apricot jam, sieved

1-egg quantity Royal icing (see page 135)

length of wire or cane, 45 cm (18 inches) long

little cotton wool or kitchen paper

3 lengths of 1.5 cm (½ inch) wide ribbons or approx 1½ metres (1½ yards) each of following colours: red, orange, blue, yellow and green

Preparation time: about 6 hours, plus cooling, setting and drying
Cooking time: about 1¼ hours
Oven: 160°C 325°F, Gas Mark 3

1. Grease and line a 20 cm (8 inch) square cake tin with greased greaseproof or non-stick silicone paper.
2. Make up the cake mixture, put into the tin and level the top. Cook in a preheated oven for about 1¼ hours for both types of cake until well risen and firm to the touch.
3. Turn out on to a wire rack and leave to cool. Leave to 'set' for 24 hours before cutting up.
4. For the cart: colour 450 g (1 lb) Fondant moulding paste a red or orange colour. Cover the outside base and sides of an 18 cm (7 inch) square cake tin with non-stick silicone paper attaching with pins if necessary. Roll out the fondant to about 5 mm (¼ inch) thick and first cut out a square to fit the base of the tin and position it. Next roll out long strips and cut out two of approx 35 × 4 cm (14 × 1½ inches). Place these around the sides of the cake tin, dampening well where they meet the base. Put to dry in a warm place for at least 48

hours or until firm enough to remove from the tin without collapsing. Stand on a cake board.
5. Colour 350 g (12 oz) Fondant moulding paste a good green, 350 g (12 oz) blue and 350 g (12 oz) yellow.
6. Trim the edges of the cake so they are quite flat and even and then cut the cake into nine 5 cm (2 inch) squares. From the trimmings cut out two more squares of the same size, sticking the pieces together with jam to get the shape and size.
7. Roll out one piece of Fondant moulding paste and cut into 8 strips of 15 × 5 cm (6 × 2 inches). Brush with sieved jam. Stand one cake square on a piece of fondant and wrap it round the cake so it encloses 3 sides. Stand the cake on another piece of fondant and fold around it to enclose the other 3 sides. Damp the edges of the fondant and press them together neatly. Repeat with the other 3 bricks in the same colour.
8. Use the other coloured fondants to cover 4 more bricks of blue and then use 275 g (9 oz) of the yellow to cover the last three bricks, in the same way. Leave to dry for at least 24 hours. Roll out the trimmings of each colour and cut out small shapes to attach to the sides of the bricks.
9. Shape the remaining Fondant moulding paste into 4 wheels of approx 3 cm (1¼ inch) diameter and leave to dry.
10. Make up the Royal icing and colour about a quarter a pale blue. Put into a piping bag fitted with a small star nozzle and pipe stars along the seams and down the sides of the blue bricks.
11. Colour a further quarter of the icing a green to contrast with the green bricks and decorate each in the same way.
12. Colour a further quarter of the icing a bright orange and use to decorate the remaining yellow bricks.
13. Colour the remaining icing a bright

yellow and put into a piping bag fitted with a small star nozzle.
14. Carefully stand the 'cart' on a cake board, attaching it with dabs of icing. Attach two wheels each side and pipe stars all around the edges of these.
15. Then pipe rows of stars down the corners of the cart and along the base and if you like, the top edge. Leave to dry.
16. Attach the various coloured shapes to the sides of the bricks with dabs of icing, making sure the colours are well mixed.
17. Bend a piece of wire or cane to make a handle for the cart. First wind cotton wool or strips of kitchen paper around the handle and secure with sticky tape, then take coloured ribbons and wind these attractively around the handle. Carefully stick the handle into the ends of the cart, attaching with icing and holding in place until set. Tie excess ribbons in bows for the handle of the cart.
18. Use the bricks to fill the cart, building them up as you like.

FROSTY THE SNOWMAN 😊😊

5-egg and 4-egg basic Quick mix cake (see pages 128-9) or Madeira cake mix (see pages 130-1) either plain, orange, lemon or chocolate flavours or a mixture of flavours

Butter cream:
50 g (2 oz) butter or margarine
100 g (4 oz) icing sugar, sifted
little lemon juice

6 tablespoons apricot jam or orange marmalade, sieved
1 kg (2 lb) Fondant moulding paste (see page 137)
wooden skewer
½ egg white quantity of Royal icing (see page 137)
liquid or paste food colourings – pink, orange, red, green and black
4–6 tablespoons desiccated coconut

Preparation time: about 5 hours, plus cooling and setting
Cooking time: about 3¼–4 hours
Oven: 160°C, 325°F, Gas Mark 3

1. Grease and line three round cake tins 18 cm (7 inch); 15 cm (6 inch) and 12.5 cm (5 inch); and grease a 600 ml (1 pint) pudding basin. Add a disc of greased greaseproof paper to the base and dust it lightly with flour.
2. Make up the cake mixes in two batches and use the larger mix to divide between the largest cake tin and the basin and the smaller mix between the other two tins.
3. Cook in a preheated oven, allowing approx 1¼–1½ hours for the largest cake; 1–1¼ hours for the next; about an hour for the smallest cake tin; and about 50 minutes for the basin, until well risen, firm to the touch and a skewer inserted in the centre comes out clean. Cool briefly in the tins then turn out carefully on to wire trays and leave until cold. Leave for at least 12

hours to 'set' before assembling.
4. Make up the Butter cream by creaming the fat until soft and then beating in the icing sugar with sufficient lemon juice to give a spreading consistency.
5. Build up the cakes, starting with the largest on a 23–25 cm (9–10 inch) round cake board. Spread with Butter cream and cover with the next layer. Spread again with Butter cream and cover with the smallest cake. Trim off the edges to give a conical shape.
6. Trim off the base of the basin cake to make it more rounded for the head.
7. Roll out 450 g (1 lb) Fondant moulding paste in a large semi-circle large enough to cover the body of the snowman. Brush the cake with jam and wrap the fondant paste around the cake, making a join at the back. Trim off around the base.
8. Roll out about 175 g (6 oz) of the remaining fondant and use to cover the head after brushing with jam; mould a nose in the correct place. Stick a wooden skewer into the body of the snowman and impale the head on top, dampening with water where the head and body meet. It is best if the head is set at a slightly off-centre angle; the skewer will hold it in place.
9. Take the trimmings from the head and body and divide in half. Mould each piece into an 'arm' about 11 cm (4½ inches) long and 2.5 cm (1 inch) wide. Attach these to the body with a little white Royal icing, moulding the arms to the correct shape. If necessary, put something under the arms to hold them in place until set, to prevent them slipping.
10. Remove about 25 g (1 oz) fondant and colour it black. Colour the remainder a deep pink or orange.
11. Roll out 75 g (3 oz) pink fondant to a long strip and cut to about 3 cm (1¼ inches) wide and 45 cm (18 inches) long. Cut into each end about 2 cm (¾ inch) to

make a fringe for the ends of the scarf and then carefully wind it around Frosty's neck, arranging the end realistically. Damp with water if it does not attach readily.
12. Use the rest of the pink fondant to make his tam-o-shanter hat. Form about 40 g (1½ oz) into a tassle, cutting into the ends with a sharp knife or scissors for the tassle effect. Roll a little icing into a narrow sausage about 1 cm (⅓ inch) in diameter and place it on his head at a jaunty angle for the rim of his hat, attaching with a little Royal icing. Roll out the remainder to a circle of approx 14 cm (5½ inch), fold the edges under and place on top of the hat rim, attaching with water, to look like a tam-o-shanter. Attach the tassle to the centre of the hat.
13. Use the black fondant icing to make two small round eyes, a smiling mouth and three black buttons. Attach all of these in the appropriate places with dabs of icing.
14. Finally colour the icing a deep green and put into a piping bag fitted with a small star nozzle. Pipe a row of stars around the tassle on the hat, around the join of the hat band and then pipe one or two rows of stars at each end of the scarf by the fringed ends. Leave to set.
15. Spoon coconut around the base of the snowman on the cake board for snow.

WOOLLY LAMB

5 or 6-egg Quick mix cake (see pages
  128-9) or Madeira cake (see pages 130-1)
5 tablespoons apricot jam, sieved
350 g (12 oz) Fondant moulding paste (see
  page 137)
liquid or paste food colourings – black,
  green and blue

Butter cream:
350 g (12 oz) butter, preferably unsalted
675 g (1½ lb) icing sugar, sifted
few drops vanilla essence
little milk or lemon juice

Preparation time: about 3 hours, plus
cooling and setting
Cooking time: about an hour
Oven: 160°C, 325°F, Gas Mark 3

1. Grease and line a roasting tin of approx
30 × 25 cm (12 × 10 inches) with greased
greaseproof paper or non-stick silicone
paper.
2. Make up the cake mixture: the larger
quantity makes a deeper cake. Put into the
tin and level the top, making sure there is
plenty of mixture in the corners.
3. Cook in a preheated oven, allowing
about 50 minutes for the 5-egg mixture
and about 10 minutes longer for the larger
cake.
4. Turn the cake out carefully on to a wire
tray and leave to cool; then leave for 12-24
hours to 'set'.
5. Trim off the top of the cake evenly and
stand upside down on a cake board.
6. Draw a shape of a lamb on a piece of
paper or card, cut it out and position on
the cake. The ears and tail may have to be
cut from the cake trimmings. Cut carefully
all round the template pattern right
through the cake. Cut out ears and tail,
position on the board and attach all to the
cake with jam. Brush the cake with jam.
7. Colour 75 g (3 oz) Fondant moulding

paste a grass green and roll out thinly; use
to cover the cake board around the lamb's
legs and body up to sky level, attaching
with jam.
8. Colour about 50 g (2 oz) fondant a sky
blue, roll out thinly and use to cover the
rest of the cake board for the sky.
9. Remove a small piece of white fondant
for the eyes and colour the remainder
black or a brownish-black. Roll out thinly
and use to cover the head and ears of the
lamb and also the legs, nearly up to the top
of the legs. Mould neatly to the cake and
trim off where it meets the grass or sky.
10. Make up the Butter cream by creaming
the butter until soft and then gradually
beat in the icing sugar and essence, adding
sufficient milk or lemon juice to give a piping consistency.
11. Put the Butter cream into a piping bag
fitted with a small vegetable star nozzle
and pipe touching stars all over the body
of the lamb to touch the black face, legs,
grass and sky, to represent the woolly fur.
12. Roll out the remaining white fondant
and cut out two almond shapes for eyes.
Attach to the head and then add 2 small
rounds of black fondant for the pupils, and
another small piece to put on top of the
black face for the nose. Mark in the nose
and mouth with a knife or cocktail stick.
Leave to set.

NOTE: If there is any Butter cream left
over a little may be coloured green and
piped into the grass for branches of daisies
and rough patches of grass. For the daisies
simply pipe a white star of icing and put a
yellow mimosa ball in the centre.

COCO THE CLOWN ☺☺☺

5-egg and 3-egg Quick mix cake (see pages 128-9) or Madeira cake mixture (see pages 130-1)

Chocolate butter cream:
50 g (2 oz) butter or margarine
75 g (3 oz) icing sugar, sifted
25 g (1 oz) cocoa powder, sifted
little milk

2 or 3 long wooden skewers
4 tablespoons apricot jam or marmalade, sieved
1 kg (2.2 lb) Fondant moulding paste (see page 137)
liquid or paste food colourings – peach, pink, yellow, red, orange, blue or purple, green and black
2 wooden cocktail sticks
1-egg quantity Royal icing (see page 135)

Preparation time: about 6 hours, plus cooling and setting
Cooking time: about 2½ hours
Oven: 160°C, 325°F, Gas Mark 3

1. Grease and line 3 round cake tins 18, 15 and 12.5 cm (7, 6 and 5 inch) with greased greaseproof paper or non-stick silicone paper and grease a 600 ml (1 pint) pudding basin. Add a disc of non-stick silicone paper to the base and dust the basin lightly with flour.
2. Make up the cake mixtures in two batches and divide the larger mixture between the largest and smallest cake tins, and the other mixture between the 18 cm (6 inch) cake tin and basin, levelling all the tops evenly.
3. Cook in a preheated oven allowing about 1¼ hours for the largest; 50–60 minutes for the middle and smallest cakes and 45–50 minutes for the basin, until well risen, firm to the touch and a skewer inserted in the centre comes out clean.

Cool briefly in the tins then turn out carefully and leave to cool. Leave for 12–24 hours to 'set' before assembling.
4. Make up the Butter cream by creaming the fat until soft then beat in the icing sugar and cocoa with sufficient milk to give a spreading consistency.
5. Build up the cakes into a clown, starting with the largest and attaching it to a 23 cm (9 inch) round cake board with Butter cream.
6. Spread the cake with Butter cream and cover with the next cake. Again spread with Butter cream and add the smallest cake. Trim off all the edges of the cakes to give an even conical shape. Make a cut at the front of the cake at the base and remove a small wedge so that the cake is divided into two 'legs'.
7. Trim off the base of the basin cake to make it more rounded for the head.
8. Attach the 'head' to the body, again with Butter cream, and then stick 2 or 3 long wooden skewers down through the head and into the body, down through to the cake board. Brush all over the cake with jam.
9. Colour 175 g (6 oz) Fondant moulding paste a flesh colour, roll out and use to cover the head, trimming off below the neck. Shape the trimmings into 2 large ears and two hands, marking fingers with a knife. Attach the ears to the head.
10. Colour 450 g (1 lb) Fondant moulding paste a bright yellow. Roll out and cut into a semi-circle large enough to wrap round the body of the clown, trimming it off at the neck and joining it at the back. Also trim off around the base, pressing into the cut at the front for the legs.
11. Divide the yellow trimmings in half and mould each into an arm. Attach the hands to the ends of the arms and then attach to the body with a cocktail stick and a dab of icing. Hold in place if necessary so

they don't slip down.
12. Colour about 40 g (1½ oz) fondant a deep orange or red. First, mould a large red knob for a nose and attach it to the face then mould out a large smiling mouth and 2 eyebrows.
13. Colour 100 g (4 oz) fondant a deep blue or purple and use to mould 2 long shoes and attach to the base of the cake at the bottom of the 'trousers'. Roll out the remainder and cut out spots of 1.5 and 2 cm (½ and ¾ inch) and attach all over the clown's clothes.
14. Colour about 100 g (4 oz) fondant a deep green colour and first cut out a bow tie. Roll out about a third of the remainder and cut into a circle of approx 6 cm (2½ inches). Roll the remainder into a ball with a flat base and attach to the hat with a dab of icing to make a bowler. Leave these to dry.
15. Cut out two large oval white clown eyes from the white fondant trimmings, two circles for the cheeks and a long oval for the mouth. Attach to the mouth with icing and then add the red mouth and eyebrows in the appropriate places.
16. Tint a tiny piece of fondant black and use to roll into two small balls to attach to the pupils for eyeballs.
17. Put the Royal icing into a piping bag fitted with a star nozzle and pipe a 'ruff' all round the neck of the clown, attaching the green bow tie at the front, then pipe a ruff around each wrist and at the bottom of the trousers.
18. Colour a little icing orange and put into a piping bag fitted with a large writing nozzle. Use to pipe a few strands of hair down the back of the head.
19. Finally, attach the bowler hat to the head of the clown at a jaunty angle and leave him to set for at least 24 hours.

RED SPIDER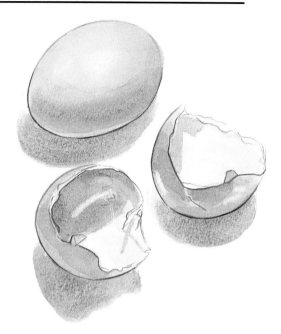

3-egg Quick mix cake, any flavour (see pages 128-9)
3 tablespoons apricot jam or marmalade, sieved
500 g (1¼ lb) Fondant moulding paste or white marzipan (see pages 136 and 137)
red paste food colouring
9 long pipe cleaners
brown or black liquid food colouring
½ egg white quantity Royal icing (see page 135)

Preparation time: about 4 hours, plus cooling
Cooking time: about 1¼ hours
Oven: 160°C, 325°F, Gas Mark 3

1. Grease a 600 ml (1 pint) ovenproof basin and an oval ovenproof glass dish of approx 25 × 19 cm (10 × 7½ inches) (capacity 900 ml/1½ pints) and put a piece of greased greaseproof paper in the base of each. Dust each lightly with flour.
2. Make up the cake mixture, flavouring it as you like, and divide between the containers so they are evenly filled (about ¾ of the way up the oval dish). Level the tops.
3. Cook in a preheated oven side-by-side standing on a baking sheet, allowing about 45 minutes for the basin and 1¼ hours for the larger cake, until firm to the touch and slightly shrinking from the sides.
4. Turn out carefully on to wire trays, leave until cold and peel off the paper.
5. Place the oval cake flat side down on an oblong board and trim a small piece from one end. Add the round cake for the head so it fits neatly on to the body.
6. Brush both pieces of cake with sieved jam but keep the head away from the body at this stage.
7. Colour the Fondant moulding paste or marzipan a deep red using red colouring paste (and remember it intensifies as it dries). Roll out two-thirds and use to cover

the body of the spider neatly. Trim off at the base.
8. Roll out the remaining fondant or marzipan and use to cover the head. Position it closely to the body, dampening slightly with water so it sticks. Trim off round the head. Make two tiny balls for the eyes and position on the head, dampening slightly so they stick.
9. If you want the legs to be red rather than be white, paint each pipe cleaner with red liquid food colouring and leave to dry. Cut one pipe cleaner in half for the antennae.
10. Colour the Royal icing a deep red so that it is a little darker than the fondant or marzipan (a spot of black or brown colouring may also be necessary to deepen the colour). Put into a piping bag fitted with a No. 1 writing nozzle.
11. Pipe alternate straight lines and wavy lines from one side of the spider to the other all along the length of it and add a couple of lines to decorate the head.
12. Paint the eyes with brown or black food colouring and mark in a mouth with a knife and then paint in with the colouring.
13. Stick the two short pieces of pipe cleaner into the head above the eyes for the antennae.
14. Make bends in the remaining pipe cleaners, as the legs in the picture. Position 3 each side, bent so they face forward and with the last pair facing backwards. Just stick them into the body lightly. If they don't stay in position, add a small dab of Royal icing.

NOTE: Spiders come in a variety of shapes and sizes as well as colours. Some can have round bodies and short legs whilst others have fairly elongated bodies and long legs, or really tiny bodies with very long thin legs. Take your pick of other shapes and colours, if you prefer.

MOUSE CLOCK

2-egg and 3-egg Quick mix cake, any
 flavour (see pages 128-9)
5 tablespoons apricot jam, sieved
900 g (2 lb) Fondant moulding paste (see
 page 137)
blue paste food colouring
1-egg quantity Royal icing (see page 135)

Preparation time: about 7 hours, plus
cooling and setting
Cooking time: about 1½ hours
Oven: 160°C, 325°F, Gas Mark 3

1. Grease and base line a 450 g (1 lb) loaf
tin and an 18 cm (7 inch) round cake tin
with greased greaseproof or non-stick silicone paper.
2. Make up the 2-egg mixture and put
three-quarters of it into the loaf tin. Put
the remainder in the round tin.
3. Make up the 3-egg mixture and add to
the mixture already in the round tin. Level
the tops and cook in a preheated oven,
allowing about 50 minutes for the loaf tin
and about 1½ hours for the round cake,
until firm to the touch and a skewer
inserted in the centre comes out clean.
4. Turn out the cakes and cool on wire
trays. Leave for at least 12 hours to 'set'.
5. Stand the loaf cake upside down so the
narrow base is upwards and cut out a gen-
tle scoop from the centre of the top of the
cake, for the round 'face' of the clock to fit
in.
6. Stand the loaf cake on an oblong board
and brush all over with sieved jam.
7. Colour all but 100 g (4 oz) of the Fondant moulding paste a pale blue. Remove
just over one-third of it and colour this a
deeper blue and wrap in polythene. Roll
out two-thirds of the pale blue icing and
use to cover the loaf cake. Mould to fit it
and then trim off evenly at the base.
8. Roll out half the deep blue icing and cut
out an 18 cm (7 inch) round to fit the face

of the clock.
9. Cut the round cake so the base and top
are both flat and brush one side with jam.
Position the 'face' carefully on it, lay the
cake on non-stick silicone paper, icing
downwards on it on a flat surface. Roll out
the other piece of dark blue to another 18
cm (7 inch) circle, brush with jam and
position on the cake.
10. Roll out the paler blue fondant and cut
a strip to fit all round the side of the cake, a
little wider so it just overlaps the edge.
Brush the sides of the cake with jam and
attach the strip, join underneath.
11. Press the icing to the cake and then
crimp the two icing edges together.
12. Put some of the white Royal icing into
a piping bag fitted with a No. 2 writing
nozzle.
13. Mark a circle on the face of the cake
about 4 cm (1½ inches) in from the edge.
Pipe a row of touching dots in white all
round on this line.
14. Pipe a continuous loop all round the
edge of the face of the clock taking each
loop in about 1.5 cm (½ inch) from the
edge. Then pipe a second looped line as
before but in between the first ones to
form an overlap.
15. Pipe the numbers on the face of the
clock and the hands of the clock facing
whatever time you like. Leave to dry.
16. Spread a little icing into the centre of
the base over the pale blue fondant and
carefully position the clock face in it so
that the numbers on the face are evenly
positioned. It may be necessary to prop it
up from behind until it sets in position.
17. Take about 40 g (1½ oz) each of the
dark blue and white fondant icing trimmings and roll each into long thin sausages
of about 5mm (¼ inch) thick, long enough
to reach around the rounded sides of the
clock. Twist these carefully together.
18. Pipe a thin line of white icing around

the pale blue side of the clock towards the
back and carefully position the twisted
rope of icing all round on top. Trim off the
ends.
19. Using the white icing and No. 2 writing
nozzle, pipe 'Happy Birthday' on the clock
base at the front and then pipe a simple
motif each side of the writing and another
one on each end of the loaf cake.
20. Pipe rows of white dots to outline the
whole of the base of the clock across the
top, down the corners and around the
base.
21. At the quarter hour figures, pipe a
design on the top of the cake of 7 graduated dots lengthwise and five crossways.
Repeat between the quarter numbers.
22. Finally, pipe a row of dots all round
the back edge of the clock face.
23. Using the rest of the dark blue fondant
trimmings mould out a 'mother' mouse
with two little ears and a tail. Mark 2 eyes
with a skewer. With the remaining white
fondant mould three 'baby' mice in the
same way. Attach to the board with icing.

COLOURED BALL 🐑🐑

3-egg basic Madeira cake mixture (see pages 130-1)
3 tablespoons apricot jam, sieved
450 g (1 lb) Fondant moulding paste (see page 137)
½-egg quantity Royal icing (see page 135)
liquid or paste food colourings – green, blue, red and orange
silver balls (optional)

Preparation time: about 3½–4 hours, plus cooling and setting
Cooking time: about 1¼ hours
Oven: 160°C, 325°F, Gas Mark 3

To make this cake it is essential to have a spherical mould used for making Christmas puddings. They are widely available or can be hired from specialist cake decorating shops. You need one for a 1 kg (2.2 lb) pudding with a diameter of 12.5 cm (5 inches). If you find a larger one then adapt the quantities accordingly. It is possible to make two semi-circular cakes in round-based basins, but they are never completely round.

1. Grease the two separate halves of the tin, place a tiny piece of greased greaseproof paper in the base of each, especially over the end with the hole; dredge the insides lightly with flour. Stand one half on its own stand on a baking sheet and rest the other one in a small pudding bowl or other ovenproof container to keep it in place.
2. Make up the Madeira mixture and divide it between the tins, spreading evenly and making sure there is sufficient around the sides.
3. Cook in a preheated oven for 1–1½ hours until well risen, firm to the touch and a skewer inserted in the centre comes out clean. Leave to cool briefly in the tin, when it should shrink back slightly from the sides. Turn on to a wire tray and leave until cold.
4. Cut the top off each cake evenly so they fit together to make a complete sphere and then sandwich together with some of the jam. Sieve the remainder and leave the cake to 'set' for at least 12 hours.
5. Colour all the Fondant moulding paste a pale green (or other colour if you like); then remove about 100 g (4 oz) and colour it a much deeper green, adding a touch of blue if necessary to darken it. Keep both separately wrapped in polythene.
6. Take a piece of string, run it from the top point of the ball to the base point and measure it (approx 20 cm/8 inches). Next run the string around the circumference of the ball, measure it and divide the amount by four, giving a length of approx 11 cm (4½ inches).
7. Draw a tall diamond using these measurements approx 20 × 11 cm (8 × 4½ inches) on card or thick paper and cut out.
8. Roll out the pale green fondant and cut out four of these diamonds. Brush the cake carefully all over with jam and mould the diamonds evenly over the ball so the four points meet at the top and base, as do the centre points of the diamonds.
9. Next, roll out the darker fondant and cut out 8 pieces to fit into the spaces in the ball – these should be approx 12.5 cm (5 inches) tall by just under 2.5 cm (1 inch) at the widest part.
10. Carefully position these strips on the ball to complete the design. Attach the ball at a slight angle to a small cake board, using the fondant trimmings and/or a little Royal icing coloured the same as the fondant. Leave for a while until the ball is firmly attached to the board and beginning to set.
11. Colour half the Royal icing an orange colour and put into a piping bag fitted with a small star nozzle. Colour the remaining icing a deep orange/red (red paste colouring gives the best colour) and put into a piping bag fitted with a No. 2 writing nozzle.
12. Using the orange icing, pipe a line around the circumference of the ball. Next, pipe 5 or 6 continuous shells centrally down the length of the dark green insets (you will not be able to reach those on the underside of the ball). Next, pipe a triangle shape towards the top or base of each pale green piece radiating out from the points where all the pieces join at the top. Add a star to the centre of each.
13. Below the triangle pipe 5 graduated stars with a space between, as in the picture. Finally, pipe a circle around the top of the ball about 4 cm (1½ inches) in diameter with a star in the centre.
14. Using the red icing, pipe a zig-zag 'V' design both sides of this line around the circumference. Pipe an outline to the triangles about 1 cm (⅓ inch) outside it and a red dot to the central star.
15. Pipe red dots between the orange stars beneath the triangles and another 'V' zigzag touching the circle at the top and/or base of the ball. Add red dots to each coloured tip where it meets at the top and also dots at each end of the orange shells on the dark green insets.
16. Silver balls may be added to some of the orange stars for extra decoration. Leave to set completely.

NOTE: Balls can be decorated in a variety of ways to represent such things as footballs, cricket balls, ten-pin bowls etc. Simply work out the pattern and size of pieces of fondant you need to cut by measuring the lengths and widths with string.

TEDDY BEARS' PICNIC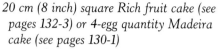

20 cm (8 inch) square Rich fruit cake (see
  pages 132-3) or 4-egg quantity Madeira
  cake (see pages 130-1)
800 g (1¾ lb) marzipan (see page 136) for
  fruit cake only
4 tablespoons apricot jam, sieved
1.5 kg (3½ lb) Fondant moulding paste (see
  page 137)
liquid or paste food colourings – green,
  pink, mauve, brown, yellow, orange
red icing pen
a little Royal icing (see page 135)

Preparation time: 5–6 hours, plus
cooling and setting
Cooking time: 1½–3½ hours
Oven: 150°C, 300°F, Gas Mark 2 or
160°C, 325°F, Gas Mark 3

1. Grease and line a 20 cm (8 inch) square
cake tin with greased greaseproof paper or
non-stick silicone paper (double thickness
for a fruit cake).
2. Make up the cake mixture and put into
the tin, levelling the top and making sure
there is plenty of mixture in the corners.
With a fruit cake make a slight hollow in
the centre and tie strips of several thicknesses of brown paper around the outside
of the tin.
3. Cook in a preheated oven, the cooler
temperature for a fruit cake, allowing
approx 3¼–3½ hours, and the higher temperature for the Madeira cake, until well
risen, firm to the touch and a skewer
inserted in the centre comes out clean.
4. Turn out on to a wire tray and leave
until cold. Trim off the top of the cake so it
is quite even, if necessary, and then stand
upside down on a 23 cm (9 inch) square
cake board.
5. For a Rich fruit cake cover it first with
marzipan. Leave for several days to set.
6. For a Madeira cake brush all over with
sieved jam, if marzipan covered, adding

touches of jam here and there to the marzipan so the Fondant moulding paste will
stick to it.
7. Colour about 450 g (1 lb) Fondant
moulding paste a grass green, roll it out
thinly and use to cover the cake completely, moulding it to fit evenly, especially over the corners. Trim off evenly
around the base of the cake.
8. Roll out about 100 g (4 oz) white fondant and cut into 18 2.5 cm (1 inch)
squares. Tint another 100 g (4 oz) fondant
a pale pink, roll out and cut into another 18
squares of 2.5 cm (1 inch).
9. Arrange the coloured squares alternately on the grass, overlapping at least 2
edges, to form the tablecloth, and dampening each lightly so they stick. Leave to
set.
10. Colour about 175 g (6 oz) fondant a
mid brown. Remove 90 g (3½ oz) and
shape into a teddy bear. First, shape a
rounded head with pointed nose and 2
rounded ears and a slight point at the neck.
Next, shape a round body, make a dip in
the top and fit the head into it. Make 2
small 'arms' and attach one each side of
the body; then make 2 rounded legs and
feet and stick them on under the body.
11. Mark 4 'toes' on both arms and feet
with a knife and make 2 eyes by piercing
with a cocktail stick, and add a mouth.
Colour a minute piece of fondant dark
brown or black and stick a small nose on to
the bear. Make a second smaller brown
bear in the same way. Leave to dry.
12. Using about 175 g (6 oz) white fondant
make two more bears as above.
13. Using 150 g (5 oz) fondant coloured a
golden yellow make another 2 small bears.
14. Using 150 g (5 oz) fondant coloured a
golden yellow/brown make 2 more small
bears. Leave them all to dry.
15. Colour about 75 g (3 oz) fondant a deep
pinky-mauve and roll out thinly. Cut out

three plates of approx 4 cm (1½ inch)
diameter and eight of just over 2 cm (¾
inch) diameter. These can be decorated
around the edge with an icing pen, if liked.
Mould 8 mugs or cups out of the same fondant.
16. Next, mould 2 or 3 honey pots out of
the same fondant and put a tiny piece of
brownish fondant on top to represent the
honey. Using an icing pen write 'Honey'
on the side of each pot.
17. Colour a little fondant a brownish
colour and use to shape into a round cake.
Cut out two wedges and put these on to
small plates. Put the cut cake on to one of
the large plates. Then make a 'loaf' cake
out of the same fondant and take some
slices off it. Put the rest of the cake and the
slices on to another of the large plates.
18. Roll out a little white fondant and cut
into small squares for sandwiches. Draw
around the outside of each with a coloured
icing pen to represent the filling. Pile these
'sandwiches' up on the last large plate.
19. Arrange the plates, mugs, honey pots
and plates of food on the tablecloth on the
cake, attaching with water or a dab of
icing.
20. Place the teddy bears around the tablecloth, some on the grass and some actually
sitting on the cloth. Either simply dampen
the base of each to attach, or add a dab of
icing to the base of each bear so it sticks
firmly, or stick a cocktail stick into the
bear, protruding at the base. This can then
be stuck into the cake to keep the bear
firmly in place.
21. Tint the Royal icing the same green as
the 'grass', put into a piping bag fitted with
a No. 3 writing nozzle and pipe strands of
icing part way up the sides of the cake,
from the base upwards, for 'grass'.

MRS RABBIT

5-egg chocolate Quick mix cake (see pages 128-9)
4 tablespoons apricot jam, sieved
450 g (1 lb) Fondant moulding paste (see page 137)
liquid or paste food colourings – brown and black

Butter cream:
300 g (10 oz) butter, preferably unsalted
500 g (1¼ lb) icing sugar, sifted
1½ level tablespoons cocoa powder, sifted
few drops vanilla essence
little milk

2–3 pieces raw spaghetti
1 metre (1 yard) deep pink satin ribbon approx 2.5 cm (1 inch) wide

Preparation time: about 3 hours, plus cooling and setting
Cooking time: about 2¼ hours
Oven: 160°C, 325°F, Gas Mark 3

1. Thoroughly grease a 900 ml (1½ pint) round pudding basin and an ovenproof bowl of approx 21 cm (8½ inch) diameter and capacity of approx 2.25 litres (4 pints) with a rounded base, then put a disc of non-stick silicone paper in the base of each.
2. Make up the cake mixture and divide between the bowls so they are evenly full. Level the tops, making sure the sides have plenty of mixture.
3. Cook in a preheated oven, allowing approx 1 hour for the basin and 1¼ hours for the bowl, or until well risen, firm to the touch and a skewer inserted in the centre comes out clean.
4. Carefully loosen the cakes from the containers and turn out on to wire racks. When cold, leave for at least 12 hours before shaping.
5. Trim off the top from both the cakes if

necessary so they stand evenly when upside down. Put the larger one on to a cake board of approx 33 × 20 cm (13 × 8 inch) and trim off a piece from each side to make it more oval and rabbit-shaped. Place the trimmings on top of the back of the rabbit, reversing them and attaching with jam, to give a more rounded shape.
6. Cut out a small semi-circle from the front of the body for the 'head' cake to fit into. Position the head, and again trim off a little piece from each side so it is slightly elongated. Attach the head with jam and then use the jam to brush all over the body and head.
7. Mould front paws from white Fondant moulding paste, using about 25 g (1 oz) for each one. Attach on each side of the rabbit as in the picture. Next, shape 2 hind legs and feet using 40–50 g (1½–2 oz) each and attach to the back of the rabbit. Also form a round 'tail' from about 40 g (1½ oz) fondant, but do not attach yet.
8. Next, roll a little fondant out and cut two ovals with pointed ends about 2.5 cm (1 inch) long for eyes and keep aside.
9. Roll out 50 g (2 oz) white fondant for the linings of the ears and cut out long ovals with a point at one end and flat edge at the other end approx 10 cm (4 inches) long.
10. Colour about 20 g (¾ oz) fondant black and keep for the pupils of the eyes and the nose.
11. Make up the Butter cream by creaming the butter until soft then gradually beat in the icing sugar, cocoa, vanilla essence and sufficient milk to give a spreading consistency. Use to spread evenly all over the rabbit, including the head, legs and paws.
12. Colour the remaining 75 g (3 oz) fondant the same colour brown as the icing. Roll out and cut out two 'outer ears', a little larger than the white ones, dampen and attach the white pieces for lining. Fold

over the edges slightly and leave to dry. Use the brown trimmings to roll out and cut out 2 small eyebrows and make cuts all along and minute rolls cut into lengths to add 3 'toes' to each foot.
13. Position the eyes on the head and then put the eyebrows just on top. Make two tiny balls or circles of black fondant for the pupils of the eyes and attach.
14. Use the remaining black fondant for a nose for the rabbit and attach 3 or 4 pieces of spaghetti each side for whiskers. Also attach the white fondant tail.
15. When quite set and dry, tie the ribbon around the rabbit's neck and complete with a big bow.

MAYPOLE CAKE 😊😊

2 × 3-egg quantities Quick mix cake,
  chocolate or coffee flavoured (see pages
  128-9)

Chocolate butter cream:
175 g (6 oz) butter or soft margarine
350 g (12 oz) icing sugar, sifted
40 g (1½ oz) cocoa, sifted
4–6 teaspoons milk

12 narrow coloured ribbons, each 1 metre in
  length (mixed colours)
35 cm (14 inches) long narrow stick (for the
  maypole)
225 g (8 oz) Fondant moulding paste (see
  page 137) or white marzipan (see page
  136)
green liquid or paste food colouring
2–2½ packets chocolate finger biscuits
approx 30 Royal icing daisies in shades of
  pink with yellow or white centres (see
  page 140)
approx 30 daisy leaves
silver or coloured ball (dragées)
8–10 moulded animals (see below)

Preparation time: about 10 hours,
including moulding animals and flowers,
plus cooling and setting
Cooking time: about 1 hour 20 minutes
Oven: 160°C, 325°F, Gas Mark 3

1. Make up the cake mixtures separately
and put each into a greased and base-lined
23 cm (9 inch) round sandwich tin.
2. Level the tops and cook in a pre-heated
oven, allowing about 30–40 minutes for
each cake, until well risen and firm to the
touch.
3. Turn out carefully on to wire trays and
leave until cold and preferably for up to 12
hours to 'set'.
4. Make up the Butter cream by beating
the butter or margarine until soft then
gradually beating in the icing sugar and

cocoa powder with sufficient milk to give a
piping and spreading consistency.
5. Use the Butter cream to sandwich the
cakes together and attach to a 30 cm (12
inch) round cake board.
6. Use more of the icing to completely
mask the whole cake with a thin layer of
Butter cream.
7. Colour the Fondant moulding paste or
marzipan a grass green. Roll out to a circle
to fit the top of the cake, position and trim
off evenly around the edge.
8. Arrange chocolate biscuits all round the
outside of the cake, so they touch each
other; cut them into even lengths so they
just appear over the top of the cake.
9. Wind two different coloured ribbons
evenly around the maypole stick, then
stick the maypole centrally into the cake.
10. Arrange daisies and leaves around the
maypole, attaching with Butter cream.
Then arrange bunches of daisies and
leaves around the edge of the cake on the
green fondant or marzipan, touching the
biscuit fence.
11. Put the rest of the Butter cream into a
piping bag fitted with a star nozzle and
pipe a border of stars around the base of
the biscuits. (To make a contrasting colour
scheme, you could use a plain Butter
cream for the star border: see page 34 or
page 137 for recipes.) Attach a silver ball to
every or alternate stars.
12. Make moulded animals to go on top of
the cake. Moulded teddy bears are
described in detail on page 24 and there
are other animals to choose from on page
141. Make about 8 animals or – if the party
is not too big! – one for each child attend-
ing it.
13. Arrange the moulded animals all
around the top of the cake at equal distance apart, attaching each lightly with
Butter cream.
14. Attach the remaining ribbons to the

top of the maypole, half-way along the
length of each, with a dab of Butter cream.
15. Top the maypole with a star of Butter
cream and then one or more silver balls, if
liked. Leave to set and dry.

HAMBURGER

4-egg plain Quick mix cake (see pages 128-9)

1.25 kg (2½ lb) Fondant moulding paste (see page 137)

liquid or paste food colourings – brown, red, black, orange, yellow and green

6 tablespoons apricot jam or marmalade, sieved

1 patterned paper plate (approx 25 cm/10 inch) or a 25 cm (10 inch) round cake board

1 teaspoon sesame seeds

Preparation time: about 4½ hours, plus cooling and setting

Cooking time: 40 minutes - 1 hour 10 minutes

Oven: 160°C, 325°F, Gas Mark 3

1. Grease and base line two 20 cm (8 inch) round sandwich tins and one 18 cm (7 inch) sandwich tin with greased greaseproof or non-stick silicone paper. Dust lightly with flour, shaking out the excess.

2. Make up the cake mixture. Add sufficient of the mixture to the smaller tin to fill it only ⅓ full and level the top. Divide the remainder between the other two tins and level the tops.

3. Cook in a pre-heated oven with the two larger tins on the top shelf and the smaller one on the lower shelf and allow approx 35–40 minutes for the larger cake and the same for the smaller one, of until well risen and firm to the touch. The small cake will take 20–25 minutes if cooked alone in the oven. Turn out on to wire trays and leave to cool.

4. Colour about 225 g (8 oz) Fondant moulding paste a brown hamburger colour using brown, black and red colourings. Colour 100 g (4 oz) fondant a deep red for the ketchup; colour 100 g (4 oz) fondant an orangey/yellow for the slice of cheese and 100 g (4 oz) green for the shred-

ded lettuce. Then colour 350 g (12 oz) fondant a pale golden brown for the crust of the bun and the remaining 225 g (8 oz) fondant a pale cream for the crumb of the bun. Wrap each separately in cling film or polythene until required.

5. Roll out just over half the brown fondant large enough to fit the base of the smallest cake and reach up the sides. Brush with jam, position the cake on top and press the fondant up the sides. Trim off at the edges. Roll out the remainder to a circle to fit the cake, brush with jam, and position on the cake. Trim the edges and press together.

6. Stand the cake on a sheet of non-stick silicone paper and press all over with fingers and finger nails to give an uneven surface. Next, take a fine paint brush and, using brown and black food colourings, paint all over the top and sides of the hamburger to make it look realistic.

7. Divide the red fondant icing into four pieces, mould out thinly with the fingers so each looks like dripping tomato ketchup. Place on the hamburger at four places so it 'drips' over the edge.

8. Take half the cream-coloured fondant and roll out to fit the top of one of the other cakes. Brush with jam and position; repeat with the remainder on the last cake.

9. Halve the light golden brown fondant and roll out large enough to cover the base and sides of the cake. Brush with jam and position on the cake, trimming the edges off evenly and pressing well together.

10. Repeat, using the remaining brown fondant and use to cover the other cake in the same way to make the other half of the bun.

11. Stand one half of the bun on a cake board or plate (a pretty paper plate is a good idea) with the creamy side upwards.

12. Roll out the orange/yellow fondant and trim to a square so each corner just over-

laps the 'bun'. Lay over the bun like a slice of processed cheese.

13. Carefully position the hamburger cake with dripping ketchup on the 'cheese' so it is at the best angle.

14. Take the green fondant icing and carefully grate it on the coarsest side of the grater. Arrange this over the burger for 'shredded lettuce' with strands hanging down in places all around the bun.

15. Finally put on the bun 'lid' by turning the remaining cake so the brown crust faces upwards. Carefully press the edges to give the bun a slightly rounded edge.

16. Lightly brush the top of the 'bun' with water and sprinkle with sesame seeds. Leave the cake to set for at least 24 hours.

WIGWAM 🐑🐑

*5-egg and 2-egg Madeira cake mixtures
(see pages 130-1) flavoured with lemon or
orange*
225 g (8 oz) fine cut marmalade
*550 g (1¼ lb) Fondant moulding paste (see
page 137)*
1-egg quantity Royal icing (see page 135)
6 long chocolate matchsticks
*liquid or paste food colourings – brown,
peach, orange, red and green*

Preparation time: about 6 hours, plus
cooling and setting
Cooking time: 3¾–4 hours
Oven: 160°C, 325°F, Gas Mark 3

1. Grease and line three round cake tins 18
cm (7 inch); 15 cm (6 inch) and 12.5 cm (5
inch) with greased greaseproof or non-
stick silicone paper.
2. Make up the Madeira cake mix in 2
batches, using the 5-egg mixture to divide
between the two larger tins and the 2-egg
mixture for the smallest tin.
3. Cook the largest cake for about 1¼–1½
hours; the middle size for 1–1¼ hours; and
the smallest for about an hour, until well
risen, firm to the touch and a skewer
inserted in the centre comes out clean.
Cool in the tins for a few minutes then
turn out and leave until cold.
4. Leave the cakes until the next day before assembling to 'firm' up slightly.
5. Trim the tops of the two larger cakes so
they are flat. Stand the largest on a cake
board and spread with marmalade. Top
with the next cake, spread with marmalade and then put the small one on top.
6. Using a sharp knife, cut the sides of the
cake to a conical shape, leaving a flat surface on the top cake of approx 5 cm (2
inch), to resemble the shape of a wigwam.
Cut out a small triangle of cake from the
front of the cake which reaches about 9 cm
(3½ inch) up the wigwam for the door

opening.
7. Sieve the rest of the marmalade and use
to brush all over the outside of the cake.
8. Colour the Fondant moulding paste to a
deep peachy/brown colour kneading in
red, peach and brown colourings. Remove
about 75 g (3 oz), wrap in polythene and
keep for the door flap.
9. Roll out the remaining fondant on non-
stick silicone paper dusted with icing sugar
and cornflour until it is large enough to
enclose the whole wigwam.
10. Carefully lay the fondant over the cake
with the help of a rolling pin, and press
and mould it to the shape of the cake.
Press the fondant into the doorway carefully and smooth down the back, cutting at
an angle to join. Trim off round the base.
11. Roll out the trimmings and put a narrow roll of fondant all round the base of
the wigwam, dampening slightly with
water to attach. Place another roll around
the top edge of the wigwam.
12. Roll out the reserved fondant for a
door cover, and attach it carefully with
water, folding it carefully back to attach to
the side of the wigwam with a slight loop
in it. Roll out any more trimmings and cut
out a circle of approx 4 cm (1½ inch) for a
symbol to attach over the door. Make
small slashes all around the edge with a
sharp knife for decoration. Set aside.
13. Mark 'joins' in the wigwam canvas with
the wooden end of a small paintbrush
then, using brown liquid food colouring,
paint a line over this join mark and then
lots of 'stitches' across the line.
14. Leave to set for several hours then
make up the Royal icing. Leave half white,
colour some green and some brown. Put
the white into a piping bag fitted with a
very small star nozzle and the other two
colours into piping bags fitted with No. 2
writing nozzles.
15. Mark a line all round the wigwam just

below the top of the door opening using a
skewer and another one about 3.5 cm (1¼
inch) below it.
16. Using green icing, work a twisted line
of loops all round the top skewer line on
the wigwam; then pipe a 'tree' design on
the lower line by starting at the base of
each tree and working a touching zigzag
line upwards to represent the tree and
then a vertical line down the centre for the
trunk. Pipe two or three almost touching
dots beside it on the line and continue with
trees and dots all the way round. Pipe one
larger tree on the symbol and a row of dots
all the way round just inside the edge.
17. Using brown icing, pipe a row of triangles all round the wigwam about 2.5 cm
(1 inch) above the twisted line and add a
green dot to the top of each triangle with a
smaller dot above that and one in the
centre of the triangle.
18. Using the white star nozzle, pipe a row
of zigzags all round the base of the wigwam, just touching the base and then
another zigzag row of green icing just
above the white.
19. Around the top of the wigwam work a
white zigzag and from each lower 'V' work
a straight line downwards of about 2 cm
(¾ inch) and then from each of these lines
work an upturned 'V'. Using brown icing
work a downward line of about 1.5 cm (½
inch) from the top of the 'V's.
20. Pipe a green dot below each of these
brown lines and another larger one and 2
smaller ones just lower than the base of the
brown 'V's. Pipe a row of brown dots
above the two base zigzags.
21. Paint the inside of the wigwam opening with dark brown liquid food colouring.
22. Stick 6 chocolate matchsticks into the
top of the wigwam for the supports.
23. Attach the symbol over the doorway
with icing and leave the cake to set.

PONY CAKE

*4-egg Quick mix cake (see pages 128-9) or
4-egg Madeira cake mixture, lemon
flavoured (see pages 130-1)
4 tablespoons lemon curd or orange
marmalade, sieved
675 g (1½ lb) Fondant moulding paste (see
page 137)
liquid or paste food colourings – green,
brown, blue, black*

*Butter cream:
100 g (4 oz) butter or margarine
225 g (8 oz) icing sugar, sifted
lemon juice*

*chocolate matchsticks sweets
brown or black liquid food colouring or
icing pens*

Preparation time: about 3 hours, plus
cooling and setting
Cooking time: about 1½ hours
Oven: 160°C, 325°F, Gas Mark 3

1. Grease and line a rectangular tin of
approx 28 × 18 × 4 cm (11 × 7 × 1½ inch)
with greased greaseproof paper or non-
stick silicone paper which comes at least
2.5 cm (1 inch) above the rim of the tin.
2. Make up the cake mixture and put into
the tin, levelling the top and making sure
there is plenty of mixture in the corners.
Cook in a preheated oven, allowing about
an hour for the Quick mix cake and 1–1¼
hours for the Madeira cake until well risen
and firm to the touch.
3. Turn out carefully on to a wire tray and
leave until cold. Peel off the paper and
trim off the top so it is even, then stand it
on a suitably sized rectangular cake board
with the base facing upwards. Brush all
over with lemon curd or sieved marmalade.
4. Colour about 175 g (6 oz) Fondant
moulding paste a pale sky blue. Roll it out

and lay over the top one-third of the cake,
giving it a slightly uneven edge. Press to
the cake evenly, especially over the corners
and down the sides. Trim off neatly
around the base of the cake.
5. Colour about 350 g (12 oz) fondant a
good grass green colour. Roll out and use
to cover the rest of the cake, making it
meet the sky evenly, and mould over the
corners and down the sides. Trim off
around the base of the cake.
6. Draw a picture of a horse jumping (or
trace it from a picture) and put on to a
piece of thick paper or thin card. Cut it out
neatly. Colour about 175 g (6 oz) fondant a
brown, bay, chestnut or other horse colour
and roll it out large enough to place the
card on. Cut carefully around the template
of the horse, remove the template and
then, even more carefully, move the horse
to the top of the cake so it is at a jumping
angle. Pick up edges in places and dampen
so the horse sticks to the cake.
7. Using a sharp knife, mark the front legs
into two with a sharp cut and do the same
with the back legs.
8. Roll out the trimmings and cut out a
strip for the mane, a tiny piece for the forelock and a flowing tail. Mark it with a knife
or wooden cocktail skewer to make it look
realistic. Attach the mane and forelock
with a dab of water, and then carefully
position and attach the tail in the same
way.
9. Make up the Butter cream and tint it a
deep green suitable for a hedge and trees.
10. Lay the chocolate matchsticks between
and beneath the horse's legs to make a post
and rail fence, cutting the matchsticks as
necessary for the correct lengths and then
attach them carefully with small dabs of
icing.
11. Put the icing into a piping bag fitted
with a star nozzle and pipe squiggly lines
and stars to make a 'hedge' each end of the

'fence' and then pipe out a shape for the
leaves of a tree behind the hedge.
12. Use the remaining green icing to pipe
uneven lengths of 'grass' up the sides of
the cake and odd patches on the top of the
cake on the grass.
13. Mark in the eye of the horse and either
add an 'eye' made from fondant icing or
paint in eyes and nostril with an icing pen.
Also mark in or paint the hooves a little
darker and add streaks of a darker colour
to the mane and tail with the same pen.
Leave to set.

NOTE: for a more ambitious horse, the
limbs and body can be partly moulded to
give it extra shape and dimensions but this
is far more difficult to do and will require
probably an extra 225 g (8 oz) of Fondant
moulding paste.

ROCKET ✦✦✦

3-egg Madeira cake mix (see pages 130-1)
6 tablespoons apricot jam
2 or 3 wooden skewers
1.25 kg (2½ lb) Fondant moulding paste
(see page 137)
liquid or paste food colourings – orange, red
and brown
1-egg quantity Royal icing (see page 135)
silver balls

Preparation time: about 4½ hours, plus
cooling and setting
Cooking time: about 1 hour
Oven: 160°C, 325°F, Gas Mark 3

1. Grease and line a 450 g (1 lb) loaf tin.
Thoroughly wash and dry two 425 g (15
oz) empty food cans then grease well and
line the bases with discs of non-stick silicone paper.
2. Make up the mixture and use to fill the
food cans no more than half full and put
the remainder into the loaf tin and level
the top.
3. Stand all the tins on a baking sheet and
cook in a preheated oven, allowing about
45 minutes for the loaf tin and 55–60
minutes for the cans, or until well risen
and firm and a skewer inserted in the
centre of each comes out clean.
4. Cool briefly in the tins and then turn out
very carefully on to a wire tray and leave to
cool. When cold leave to 'set' for 12-24
hours.
5. Trim the end of one of the can cakes to a
point tapering it off to halfway down the
cake. Cut both ends of the other can cake
straight and stick to the pointed one with
jam. If necessary stick 2 or 3 wooden skewers through the two cakes to keep them together and straight.
6. Stand the loaf cake base upwards and
then taper off one end from halfway along
the top to about 2.5 cm (1 inch) from the
base. Attach this piece to the other end of

the cake with jam, reversing it so it gives a
sloping 'launch pad'.
7. Sieve the remaining jam and use to
brush all over the launch pad and the
rocket.
8. Take 300 g (10 oz) white Fondant
moulding paste and roll it out to a rectangle large enough to cover the sides of
the rocket (not the pointed tip) approx 24
× 15 cm (9½ × 6 inch). Wrap around the
cake and join neatly. Roll out 50 g (2 oz)
white fondant and use for a circle to fit the
base of the rocket.
9. Roll out a circle of white fondant of
approx 12.5 cm (5 inch) using about 150 g
(5 oz) fondant. Make one cut to the centre
and position it over the pointed end of the
rocket, trimming off the excess at one side
so it fits neatly. Allow it to overlap slightly
and mark this edging into pointed crimps
with your fingers and thumb.
10. Colour about 350 g (12 oz) fondant to a
palish orange. Divide into five and shape
each into a cylinder of approx 10 cm (4
inch) and then shape the end of each into a
point.
11. Colour 150 g (5 oz) fondant a deeper
orange and roll out thinly. Cut 3 strips of
approx 24 × 2 cm (9½ × ½ inch), dampen
each slightly and wrap one around the bottom of the large cylinder, one half way up
and one just below the crimped edge.
12. Next, cut out 14–16 narrow strips of
approx 4 cm × 5 mm (1½ × ¼ inch).
Damp these and attach to the pointed end
of the rocket beginning at the base – they
should not reach the point and there
should be a gap at the base and be touching when they get near the point.
13. Colour the remaining 175 g (6 oz) fondant a brown colour. Roll out and use to
cover the launch pad, laying over the cake
and moulding it to fit the cake. Trim off
the corners and around the base.
14. Make up the Royal icing and use a few

dabs to stick the launch pad to a small loaf
cake board. Leave to set.
15. Colour about three-quarters of the
icing a deep orange and put into a piping
bag fitted with a small star nozzle. Use to
outline the launch pad angles with rows of
shells and then all around the base.
16. Pipe horizontal lines of stars or shells
along the sides of the launch pad and then
change to a No. 2 writing nozzle and add
some dots and lines in between as in the
picture.
17. On the rocket, using the star nozzle,
pipe five rows of stars or shells from one
end of the cylinder to the other evenly
around the rocket but not going over the
orange bands. Then pipe a smaller line between each.
18. Pipe a series of stars down the length of
the five individual rockets and decorate
with 2 or 3 silver balls at each end and on
the points of each rocket together with
several stars.
19. Attach 5 silver balls touching each
other on the pointed nose of the rocket between the coloured strips and pipe stars
around the nose itself.
20. Tint the remaining icing a paler orange
and put into a piping bag fitted with a
small star nozzle. Add a band of shells or
stars around the orange bands on the
cylinder of the rocket and around the base
of the rocket. Pipe a few stars on the back
end of the rocket, decorated with silver
balls.
21. Finally, attach the 5 rockets evenly
around the main rocket between the lines
of piping and to within about 2 cm (¾
inch) of the end, using orange icing. Set
aside to dry and set firmly.
22. When the rockets have set to the main
rocket, lay it on the launch pad so the nose
overlaps the end and attach with icing.
Leave to set.

ELECTRONIC KEYBOARD

2 × 3-egg Quick mix cake (see pages 128-9)
225 g (8 oz) apricot jam, sieved
1 kg (2¼ lb) Fondant moulding paste (see page 137)
liquid or paste food colourings – black, green, blue, orange, brown
1-egg quantity Royal icing (see page 135)
few sugar-coated chocolate buttons

Preparation time: about 6 hours
Cooking time: about 1¼ hours
Oven: 160°C, 325°F, Gas Mark 3

1. Make up the two cake mixtures separately and spread each into a rectangular tin of approx 28 × 18 × 4 cm (11 × 7 × 1½ inch) lined with greased greaseproof or non-stick silicone paper.
2. Cook in a preheated oven for about 40 minutes or until well risen and firm to the touch.
3. Turn the cakes out carefully on to wire trays and leave until cold.
4. Trim the cakes so they fit together neatly at the narrow ends then place upside down on a large cake board or two boards stuck together. Stick the cakes together with a little jam and then use the remaining jam to brush all over the cake.
5. Remove 75 g (3 oz) of the Fondant moulding paste and colour it black. Remove a further 225 g (8 oz) and keep it white. Colour 50 g (2 oz) fondant an orange/brown colour and colour the remaining fondant icing a mid-green. Remove 100 g (4 oz) of the green fondant and colour it a deeper green by adding both green and blue colouring to it.
6. Roll out the mid-green fondant large enough to cover the whole cake. Use to cover it making neat cuts at the corners so they fit neatly.
7. Mark a line along the top of the cake to within 2.5 cm (1 inch) of each end and one-third from one long edge (approx 6 cm/2½ inches). Roll out the white fondant to a rectangle to fit into the larger marked area leaving a 2.5 cm (1 inch) margin at each end and 1.5 cm (½ inch) margin along the long edge. Trim.
8. Position on the cake, attaching in places with sieved jam. Mark a line along the length of the white fondant just over 1.5 cm (½ inch) wide; then, using a sharp knife, mark the white rectangle into 29 white notes.
9. Roll out the black fondant and cut into 20 black notes of approx 7 × 1.5 cm (2½ × ½ inch). Attach these over the marked lines of the white notes as follows: on the first 2 lines then miss one; then next 3 lines, miss one; next 2 lines, miss one; next 3 lines, miss one: next 2, miss one; next 3, miss one; next 2 then miss one and the next 3.
10. Roll out the dark green fondant and cut a strip long enough to reach along the length of the front of the keyboard approx 2 cm (¾ inch) deep. Also cut a piece to fit along each end of the keyboard of the same width. Next, cut out rectangles of approx 7.5 × 4 cm (3 × 1½ inch) and 4 × 4 cm (1½ × 1½ inch). Position these on the green part of the keyboard at each end and mark a criss-cross design on each with a knife.
11. Mark the rest of the light green into 6 portions of the following sizes: beginning from the left: 10 cm (4 inch); 7.5 cm (3 inch); 8 cm (2½ inch); 8 cm (2½ inch); 5 cm (2 inch); 5 cm (2 inch).
12. Roll out the orange/brown fondant and cut out 11 rectangles of approx 2.5 × 1 cm (1 × ½ inch). Attach 4 to the first area, as in the picture; two to the left side of the second area; two to the third and fourth areas and one to the last area, all as in the picture.
13. Next, cut out two circles of the same colour of approx 2 cm (¾ inch); two of 1 cm (½ inch) and one of almost 2.5 cm (1 inch). Add the largest to the fifth area; and the two larger and smaller ones to the second area as in the picture.
14. Pick out 4 chocolate buttons of the same colour to add to the first area for knobs on the coloured rectangles; two more of another colour for the third area; two more for the fourth area and one for the sixth area. Stick one button into the middle of the circle in the fifth area, pointed end downwards, for the 'on and off' knob.
15. Colour the Royal icing a mid-brown and put some into a piping bag fitted with a fine writing nozzle (No. 1).
16. At the top of the first area write CHORD and below it MANUAL and BASE and the other markings as in the picture. In the next area write RHYTHM at the top and complete as in the picture. In the third put MANUAL and complete all the areas as in the picture.
17. At the top of each white note write the letters, as on an electronic keyboard, beginning with C D E F G A B and continuing to the end, which should be C.
18. Transfer the icing to a piping bag fitted with a small star nozzle and pipe a line of shells decoratively along the front and sides of the keyboard. Leave to set.

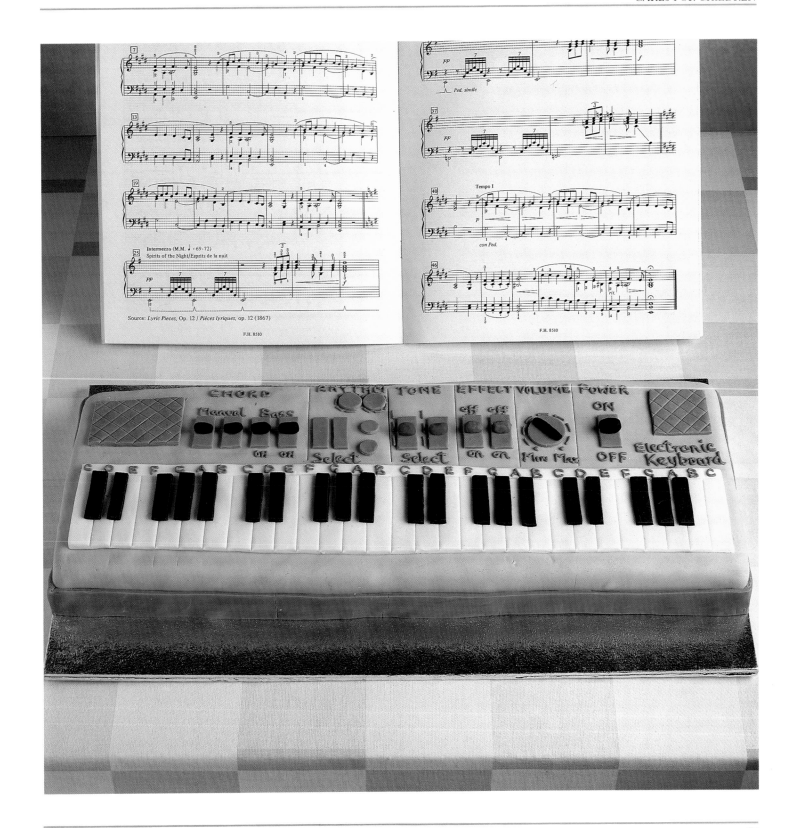

TYKIE THE TORTOISE

3-egg chocolate Quick mix cake (see pages 128-9)
3 tablespoons apricot jam, sieved
450 g (1 lb) Fondant moulding paste (see page 137)
liquid or paste food colouring – green, blue, brown, black and yellow
½-egg white quantity Royal icing (see page 135)

Preparation time: about 4 hours
Cooking time: about 1¼ hours
Oven: 160°C, 325°F, Gas Mark 3

1. Grease a 1.75–2 litre (3–3½ pint) oven-proof bowl (a mixing bowl gives the best shape), put a greased disc of greaseproof paper in the base and dust the inside lightly with flour.
2. Make up the cake and spread evenly into the bowl so there is plenty of mixture around the sides. Cook in a preheated oven for 1–1¼ hours, until well risen and firm to the touch. Cool briefly in the bowl, when the cake should begin to shrink just from the sides. Make sure the cake is loose and turn out on to a wire tray. Leave until cold.
3. Transfer the cake to a cake board, turning it upside down. Trim off about 2.5 cm (1 inch) from each side of the cake, rounding the edge off because a tortoise is a little more oval than round.
4. Cut out a small 'V' from the front of the cake for the head to be positioned, and two 'V's evenly at the front sides for front feet and two at the back of the body for the back feet. Brush the cake all over with jam.
5. Take just over 100 g (4 oz) of the fondant and colour it a greenish/brown or minty type of green (poetic licence allows for this tortoise to have a greener head and feet than normal!).
6. Use about one-third of it to mould into a head with a thick neck. Shape the end of

the neck into a slight point and position it carefully into the 'V' cut in the body for the head. The head can be moulded so it is just off the ground by laying it over a piece of cotton wool, but it is not easy to keep it off the board when the cake is moved. Mark two eyes in the head with a skewer and a deep cut for the mouth.
7. Divide the remaining green fondant into four equal pieces and shape each into reptile-like feet, again with a slight point away from the toes. Position carefully in the leg holes and then mark four toes on each foot with a sharp knife.
8. Remove about 20 g (¾ oz) from the remaining fondant and colour it yellow. Shape into a dandelion head, cutting the ends open with a knife or pair of scissors. A nearly opened flower is easier to make than a wide open one. Use a little green fondant for the calyx and attach to the flower head. Paint a wooden cocktail stick green and impale into the calyx for a stem. Leave to dry.
9. Colour the remaining fondant with green, brown and a touch of blue and black to give it a murky type of greenish-grey quite noticeably darker than the head and legs of the tortoise. It can be left a little streaky as a real tortoise shell has a mixture of colourings.
10. Roll out to an oval that is large enough to cover the cake.
11. Carefully lift and position over the cake. Make cuts over the feet and around the head, then trim the fondant so it just overlaps on to the board. Carefully mould the edges of the 'shell' so it becomes thinner and also turn it up slightly. Place a thin roll of cotton wool beneath it whilst it dries.
12. Take a fairly blunt skewer and mark uneven circles, squares and other shapes all over the shell so they all touch and make a pattern, as on a real tortoise. They

should be deep enough to be easily visible but not cut right through the icing.
13. Make up the Royal icing and colour it a deep brown with a touch of green added to it. Put into a piping bag fitted with a No. 2 writing nozzle.
14. In each marked shape on the shell, beginning on the tortoise's back, work an uneven continuous round/square Swiss-roll shape, starting at the centre and working almost to the edge of the marked shape. Repeat all over the shell.
15. Place the dandelion in front of the tortoise on the board, attaching with a dab of icing. Leave to dry.

TRANSFORMING ROBOT 😊😊

3-egg Quick mix cake (see pages 128-9)
1 kg (2¼ lb) Fondant moulding paste (see pages 137)
liquid or paste food colourings – black, mauve, red and/or orange
6 tablespoons apricot jam, sieved
1 wooden cocktail stick
1-egg quantity Royal icing (see page 135)
2 long wooden skewers

Preparation time: about 6 hours, plus cooling and setting
Cooking time: about 50–60 minutes
Oven: 160°C, 325°F, Gas Mark 3

1. Grease and line a rectangular tin 28 × 18 × 4 cm (11 × 7 × 1½ inch) with greased greaseproof paper or non-stick silicone paper. Wash and dry an empty 425 g (15 oz) food can, grease thoroughly and line the base with non-stick silicone paper.
2. Make up the cake mixture and half fill the can; put the remainder into the other tin, levelling the top and making sure there is plenty in the corners.
3. Cook in a preheated oven, allowing about 50 minutes for the can and 45–50 minutes for the rectangular cake. Test the can cake with a skewer to check it comes out clean.
4. Turn the cakes out carefully on to a wire tray and leave until cold. Leave for 24 hours to 'set' before assembling.
5. Trim the can cake evenly, then cut off a 2.5 cm (1 inch) slice. Cut this in half crosswise to make two rockers.
6. Trim the rectangular cake and then cut it neatly to give two pieces 7 cm (2½ inch) wide; one 9 cm (3½ inch) wide and the last piece 4 cm (1½ inch) wide. Cut one of the 7 cm (2½ inch) pieces and the smallest piece in half crossways to give 6 pieces and then cut one of the 6 × 7.5 cm (2½ × 3 inch) pieces in half again.
7. Colour 550 g (1¼ lb) Fondant moulding

paste a mid-grey; 350 g (12 oz) fondant a deep mauve and about 100 g (4 oz) fondant a bright red or orange.
8. Stand the largest piece of cake on a rectangular board and put the slightly smaller piece on top; brush all over the cake with sieved jam. (Cover these two pieces with fondant together, but cover the other pieces separately.)
9. Roll out some of the grey fondant and cut a strip approx 15 cm (6 inch) wide and long enough to stretch all over the cake. Position it and mould it to fit. Cut pieces to fit the ends, dampen and position.
10. Next, roll out more grey fondant and use to cover the 4 small rectangles, after brushing with jam. Leave to dry.
11. Form the grey fondant trimmings into a cylinder just the width of the can cake. Stick a cocktail stick through the length of it and leave to dry.
12. Using the mauve fondant, cover the two semicircles, the cylinder and remaining rectangle, after brushing the cake with jam. Leave to dry.
13. From the mauve fondant trimmings cut out a rectangle with pointed top large enough to fit in front of the large grey block and stand above it. Leave to set.
14. Using the red fondant icing, mould two small 'lamps'.
15. Make up the Royal icing and colour most of it grey to match the fondant by adding a little black colouring. Put into a piping bag fitted with a small star nozzle.
16. Pipe shells or stars around the ends of the main part of the robot and then a base line to attach it to the board and another line about 2.5 cm (1 inch) above it.
17. Stand the mauve rectangle on the end of this grey piece, attaching with icing and pipe a line all around the base and up the corners. Leave to set.
18. Attach the flat pointed mauve piece of fondant to the front of the block and then

put the mauve cylinder in front of it so that it touches; attach with icing. Next attach the 2 semi-circular rockers one at each side of the cylinder. Pipe a row of stars around the top front of the cylinder and a zigzag line around the base. Leave all to set.
19. Take the 2 larger grey pillars and lay on the mauve block as in the picture, attaching with icing. Pipe a base and top border of stars or shells around the upright one, join up the base decoration to the corners, and also around the ends of the flat one. Pipe a decoration on the sides of the mauve shape and leave to set.
20. Stand the two remaining grey pillars on the mauve rockers, attaching with icing, then pipe a base border and top border to each of stars or shells, a straight line down the inner edge and a motif on the front of each. Attach a red 'lamp' to the top of each with icing and lay the grey thin cylinder across these two pillars, again attaching with icing.
21. Colour the remaining icing black and put into a piping bag fitted with a No. 2 writing nozzle. Use to decorate the transformer with straight lines, dots and zigzags. Leave to set.

dear Mark
I can/can't come to your party.
from Daniel

I can't
from Peter

THUNDERCATS ☺☺☺

4-egg orange Quick mix cake (see pages 128-9)
4 tablespoons orange marmalade or any type of jam
6 tablespoons apricot jam, sieved
1.25 kg (2½ lb) Fondant moulding paste (see page 137)
liquid or paste food colouring – orange, red, blue, black, brown and green
2–3 tablespoons Royal icing (see page 135)
coloured icing pens: black and red
4–5 long wooden skewers
3 wooden cocktail sticks
little kitchen foil

Preparation time: about 5 hours, plus cooling and setting
Cooking time: about 1 hour 20 minutes
Oven: 160°C, 325°F, Gas Mark 3

1. Grease and base line three 20 cm (8 inch) round sandwich tins.
2. Make up the cake mixture and divide between the tins, levelling the tops.
3. Cook in a preheated oven, allowing 35–40 minutes. Turn out on to wire racks and cool. Leave for 12–24 hours to 'set'.
4. For the Thundercat – Lion-o: colour 175 g (6 oz) Fondant moulding paste a bright orange; about 50 g (2 oz) bright red; 25 g (1 oz) light brown; 50 g (2 oz) light blue and 50 g (2 oz) dark blue. The whole finished figure should be about 18 cm (7 inch) tall.
5. Take the orange fondant and mould a head with a nose and chin; a body; two legs but no boots or feet and 2 arms but with no hands. Press 2 thin wooden skewers up through the legs into the body to hold them in place, attaching the legs after dampening with water. Put another piece of skewer into the neck to attach and hold the head in place.
6. Use the light brown fondant for 2 small circles for the eye hollows, and a piece to

cover the mouth and chin. Also mould a hand and wrist and attach to the right arm. Mark the fingers.
7. Take the red fondant and mould a large 'glove' claw and attach to the other arm, again marking in the fingers. Mould the remainder for unruly 'hair' and attach to the head, then mark into strands.
8. Make white fondant eyeballs and position, and outline each eye with a black icing pen; mark a pupil in the centre. Outline the eyebrows and make a mouth with a red icing pen.
9. Roll out the light blue fondant and cut out a 'suit' with shoulder straps. Damp lightly and position as in the picture; turn over carefully and complete on the back. With a knife, make a mark all round the edge of the suit just in from the edge.
10. Roll a small piece of dark blue fondant into a strip and cut to shape for a belt. Position around his waist.
11. Divide the remaining dark blue in half and mould each piece into a high boot with a raised piece just below the knee. Damp the top of each and attach to the leg with the skewer going right through and having at least 2.5 cm (1 inch) protruding below the boot.
12. Lay the thundercat on a sheet of non-stick silicone paper. Darken a piece of brown fondant and cut a circle for the centre of the belt. Dampen, position and then leave the whole model to set and dry for at least 2 days in a warm place.
13. Meanwhile colour the remaining fondant (approx 800 g/1¾ lb) to a deep green with added blue and leave it streaky.
14. Stand one layer of cake on a 23 cm (9 inch) round cake board, cover with jam and add a second cake. Cut out a wedge from the top layer about two-thirds of the way back, about 2.5 cm (1 inch) wide and long enough for the other cake to fit into when standing up. Brush the cake with jam.

15. Roll out 350 g (¾ lb) fondant and use to cover the cake completely and to hang down over the edge of the board. Trim off around the base and cut into the hole in the top of the cake.
16. Roll out 175 g (6 oz) fondant and place the other single cake on it, overlapping by at least 2.5 cm (1 inch). Brush the top and sides with jam.
17. Next, roll out another 175 g (6 oz) green fondant and lay over the cake, again overlapping it well. Pinch the edges together unevenly. Stand the cake up, add a little icing and stick it upright into the hole in the cake. Stick 2 wooden skewers into it at the back for extra stability.
18. Pinch the edges pieces of overlapping fondant roughly to stand up in rocky positions all around.
19. Shape the remaining fondant into rocky mounds and attach to the 'cave' as in the picture. Leave to set thoroughly.
20. Use the white Royal icing in a piping bag fitted with a No. 2 writing nozzle to outline the top of Lion-o's boots and his belt and pipe a circle around the brown central motif of his belt.
21. Using a brown icing pen, mark 3 dots each side of the central motif on the belt. With a black icing pen, draw a lion's head with open mouth on the brown circle.
22. Attach Lion-o to the cake by putting a dab of icing under each boot and sticking the skewers firmly into the cake through the icing. Hold in position until set.
23. For his sword, use 2 cocktail sticks together and a small piece across the top, all covered in foil. Use any red fondant trimmings to cover the handle.

BAT 4 BAT 8
30   7
Total
132
for 6 WKTS
Home Team 167

Congratulations

50
50

SPORTS AND PASTIMES

Hearty outdoor activities and quieter indoor pursuits are both celebrated here. There is a lively array of cakes with sporting themes, ranging from cricket and skiing to ballooning and tennis. And there are cakes, including a word puzzle cake and a card game cake, suited to the more contemplative.

Clockwise from left: Village Cricket (see page 54), Ski-ing Cake (see page 64), Vintage Racing Car (see page 50)

HOT AIR BALLOON 🎈🎈

5-egg Quick mix cake, any flavour (see
  pages 128-9); or Madeira cake mix (see
  pages 130-1)
4 tablespoons apricot jam or marmalade,
  sieved
800 g (1¾ lb) Fondant moulding paste (see
  page 137)
liquid or paste food colourings – red, blue
  and brown
1-egg quantity Royal icing (see page 135)
4 or 6 long wooden skewers

Preparation time: about 4½ hours, plus
cooling, setting and drying
Cooking time: about 1½ hours
Oven: 160°C, 325°F, Gas Mark 3

1. Thoroughly grease an ovenproof bowl
of approx 23 cm (9 inch) diameter and
2.25 litres (4 pints) capacity. Put a disc of
non-stick silicone paper in the base and
dredge the bowl lightly with flour.
2. Make up the cake mixture and put into
the bowl, spreading it out so there is
plenty of mixture around the edges.
3. Cook in a preheated oven for 1 hour and
20–30 minutes until well risen, firm to the
touch and a skewer inserted in the centre
comes out clean.
4. Turn out on to a wire tray to cool. Leave
to set for 24 hours.
5. Stand the cake upside down on a rectangular board approx 38 × 25 cm (15 × 10
inch). Brush all over with jam.
6. Take about 100 g (4 oz) Fondant moulding paste and mould a piece to put at the
base of the round cake to make it more
elongated for the balloon. Next, take
another 100 g (4 oz) fondant and mould it
to the top of the cake so it has a good
rounded shape.
7. Three ridges can be cut out of the balloon from top to base, but it is not totally
necessary and does make covering the
cake a lot more difficult.

8. Colour 175 g (6 oz) fondant a bright blue
and another 175 g (6 oz) fondant a bright
red.
9. Roll out 100 g (4 oz) white fondant icing
and cut into a strip about 9 cm (3½ inch)
wide. Lay this over the balloon so it is just
above centre. Press to attach to the cake
and trim off neatly at the base.
10. Roll out the blue fondant and cut out a
piece to fill the centre half of the upper section of cake; and also one heart shape of
approx 5 cm (2 inch) diameter (to fit into
the white section).
11. Attach the blue piece to the top of the
balloon and trim it off around the base.
Attach the heart shape to the centre of the
white strip.
12. Roll out the red fondant and cut out
two pieces to fit into the gaps on the upper
part of the balloon and then cut out a piece
to fit the central portion of the lower part
of the balloon. Cut out two red hearts and
position on the white fondant each side of
the blue heart.
13. Roll out the rest of the blue fondant
and cut out pieces to fill the two remaining
gaps.
14. For the basket, colour 100 g (4 oz) fondant a brown basket colour. Roll out and
cut out two squares of 5 cm (2 inch) and 3
rectangles 5 × 2.5 cm (2 × 1 inch). Place
all of these on non-stick silicone paper and
leave to dry in a warm place for at least 24
hours.
15. When dry, carefully remove the pieces
of fondant. Colour the Royal icing the
same colour brown and put into a piping
bag fitted with a basket weave (ribbon)
nozzle and another fitted with a No. 2
writing nozzle. First stick the basket together with icing and leave to set.
16. For the basket weave: first pipe 1 cm (½
inch) lengths using the basket weave nozzle, under each other but leaving the width
of the nozzle between each. Next, pipe a

straight line vertically at the end of the
lines. Then, with the basket weave nozzle,
pipe another series of lines, the same
length but in between the first ones and
beginning halfway along the band of icing,
going over the vertical line and continuing
an equal distance the other side. Pipe
another vertical line at the end of these
and continue to build up the basket weave
around two short sides and 1 long side of
the basket.
17. Attach to the cake board, when dry,
about 5 cm (2 inch) below the balloon,
then work basket weave over the base of
the basket in the same way.
18. Take 4 or 6 lengths of wooden skewer
and attach the balloons to the basket by
sticking them into the side of the basket
and into the cake.
19. Names may be piped on to the balloon
itself, using a No. 2 writing nozzle.

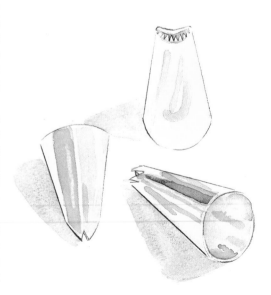

VINTAGE RACING CAR (1950s)

2 × 3-egg Quick mix cakes (see pages 128-9) or Madeira cake mix (see pages 130-1)
4 tablespoons apricot jam, sieved
1 kg (2 lb) Fondant moulding paste (see page 137)
liquid or paste food colourings – yellow and black
½-egg quantity Royal icing (see page 135)
wooden cocktail sticks

Preparation time: about 5 hours, plus cooling and setting
Cooking time: about 1¾ hours
Oven: 160°C, 325°F, Gas Mark 3

1. Grease and line two rectangular tins approx 28 × 18 × 4 cm (11 × 7 × 1½ inch) with greased greaseproof paper or non-stick silicone paper.
2. Make up the cakes separately and put each into a tin, making sure they are level and there is plenty of mixture in the corners.
3. Cook in a preheated oven, allowing 45–50 minutes for each cake, making sure it is well risen and firm to the touch.
4. Turn out on to a wire tray and cool; then leave to 'set' for 24 hours.
5. Cut a piece 11 cm (4½ inch) wide from the length of one piece of cake and a piece 10 cm (4 inch) wide from the length of the other, and sandwich together with jam. Trim both of the ends to about 6.5 cm (2¾ inch), rounding it off from about 6 cm (2½ inch). Reserve the trimmings.
6. Add a piece of the trimmings to one end making it about 4 cm (1½ inch) longer and trimming it to about 4 cm (1½ inch) at the end.
7. Mark a line halfway across the car and cut out a piece 5 cm (2 inch) wide and right through the top layer of cake.
8. On the front of the car (the smaller piece) cut out a ridge all round the front of

about 2 cm (¾ inch), tailing it off at the sides about 7.5 cm (3 inch) back. Also, slightly taper off the bonnet from the seat to the front.
9. The back of the car needs to be built up so it is about 2.5 cm (1 inch) higher than the front, using some of the cake trimmings and attaching with jam; tailing it off to a rounded point about 2 cm (¾ inch) from the tail and again cutting another ridge out of each side, as in the picture.
10. From the rest of the cake trimmings cut out two wheels of approx 5 cm (2 inch) diameter and two more of 6 cm (2½ inch) in diameter. Make sure the smaller wheels are about two-thirds the width of the large ones.
11. Brush all over the car and wheels with jam.
12. Colour 550 g (1¼ lb) Fondant moulding paste a bright lemon yellow. Roll out and use to cover the entire car, moulding it to all the undulations but cutting out a piece over the seat so it doesn't split. Trim off neatly all round the base.
13. Colour 225 g (8 oz) fondant black. Roll out and use a piece to fit inside the seat area of the car.
14. Use more black fondant to cover completely the four tyres.
15. Roll out the trimmings and use to cut out a steering wheel of approx 5 cm (2 inch) in diameter and also an anti-roll bar to fit behind the seat. Also mould two small wing mirrors. Put all of these to dry on non-stick silicone paper.
16. Roll out the remaining black trimmings thinly and cut out three 5s and three 0s for the numbers, each about 4 cm (1½ inch) tall. Attach these to the car, one pair on the bonnet and one each side of the back of the car. Also cut out an oval of about 4 × 2 cm (1½ × ½ inch) for the radiator grill and fit to the front of the car, dampening with water.

17. As the tyres begin to set use a sharp knife to mark 'treads' on them.
18. Colour about 75 g (3 oz) fondant a fairly dark grey. Roll out and use to make a seat in the car with a rounded back. Also cut out circles to fit inside the tyres; attach these with dabs of icing. Also cut out a criss-cross to fit on to the steering wheel.
19. Colour the Royal icing a lighter grey than the fondant and put into a piping bag fitted with a No. 1 or No. 2 writing nozzle. Use to pipe spokes over the grey part of the wheel out to the tyres. Leave to set.
20. Using grey icing, attach the steering wheel to the correct place and also the back anti-roll bar behind the seat and the two wing mirrors.
21. Attach the four wheels to the car with the smaller ones in front. Do not let them quite touch the car. Add dabs of icing and then put cocktail sticks into the car to hold the wheels in place and dabs of icing on to the board to hold the wheels as it sets. The wheels may need something to hold them in place whilst they set.
22. Finally, pipe lines for the radiator openings behind the car doors and a few lines down the front of the radiator grill. Leave to dry.

NARROW BOAT 🍞🍞

6-egg Quick mix cake (see pages 128-9) or
  Madeira cake mix (see pages 130-1) or a
  25 cm (10 inch) square Rich fruit cake
  mix (see page 132-3)
5 tablespoons apricot jam, sieved
100 g (4 oz) Fondant moulding paste or
  marzipan (see pages 136-7)
675 g (1½ lb) marzipan (for fruit cake
  only)
1 kg (2¼ lb) Fondant moulding paste (see
  page 137)
liquid or paste food colourings – green,
  black, red and yellow
½-egg quantity Royal icing (see page 135)
few cocktail sticks
coloured thread

Preparation time: about 4½ hours, plus
cooling and setting
Cooking time: 1–3½ hours
Oven: 150°C, 300°F, Gas Mark 2; or
160°C, 325°F, Gas Mark 3

1. Grease and line a roasting tin of approx
30 × 25 cm (12 × 10 inch) with greased
greasproof paper or non-stick silicone
paper. Double line for a fruit cake.
2. Make up the cake mix and put into the
tin, levelling the top and making sure
there is plenty of mixture in the corners.
3. Cook in a preheated oven at the lower
temperature for the fruit cake, allowing
about 3–3½ hours; or at the higher temperature for the other cakes, allowing
about an hour, or until a skewer inserted in
the centre comes out clean.
4. Turn out on to a wire tray and leave to
cool; then leave to set for 24 hours.
5. Trim off the cake so the long sides are
completely straight and even, then cut in
half lengthwise so one piece is about 2.5
cm (1 inch) wider than the other. This
makes a cake or boat rather wider than a
true narrow boat, but you need plenty of
cake to eat. Slightly round one end of the

wider piece of cake for the stern and stand
on a cake board of approx 38 × 23 cm (15
× 9 inch).
6. Cut about 7.5 cm (3 inch) off one end of
the other piece of cake and cut this piece to
make a point for the bow of the boat. Position, joining it with jam. Then brush the
cakes all over with jam. Take the 100 g (4
oz) fondant or marzipan and use to mould
the front of the boat (the bow) so it is
higher than the rest of the boat and also
has a slight wall around the edge. Fill in
any gaps in the bow where it joins the rest
of the cake so it will cover evenly.
7. If this is a fruit cake, cover both pieces of
cake with marzipan, all round the sides of
the larger piece so it overlaps the top edge
to about 2.5 cm (1 inch) at the sides and 10
cm (2 inch) at the stern. Cover the top and
sides of the smaller piece of cake.
8. Colour 550 g (1¼ lb) fondant a bright
green. Roll out part of it and use to cover
the sides of the base of the boat, taking it at
least 2.5 cm (1 inch) over the edge at the
sides, 10 cm (4 inch) at the front (over the
bow) and 5 cm (2 inch) at the stern. Pinch
up slightly all round to make a slight wall
all around the edge of the boat.
9. Next, colour about 175 g (6 oz) fondant
black, roll out and cut out two long strips
of about 2.5 cm (1 inch) wide with the
front end widening to about 4 cm (1½
inch) for the bow.
10. Dampen lightly with water and attach
to the boat over the green icing, so it is
touching the board all round.
11. Colour 175 g (6 oz) fondant a bright
red. Roll out and use to cover the sides of
the smaller piece of cake. Trim and then
place on top of the base of the boat.
12. Roll out the rest of the green fondant
and use to cover the top of the cake for a
roof, making it slightly larger all round so
the edge can be crimped with the fingers
and thumb and made to protrude slightly

over the edge of the cake.
13. Cut out a door for both the front and
back of the boat, mark in a window with a
knife and attach to the boat by dampening
with water.
14. Roll out 75 g (3 oz) white or pale grey
fondant and cut out 6 windows of approx 4
× 2.5 cm (1½ × 1 inch) and three of 2.5
cm (1 inch) square.
15. Colour a little of the icing a grey colour
and put into a piping bag fitted with a No.
2 writing nozzle. Pipe an outline to each
window and a line across the top, as in the
picture. When the icing is dry attach the
windows to the sides of the cabin of the
boat with 2 large windows, then the small
one and then another large one, on each
side; leave the same amount of space between each for decoration.
16. Colour the rest of the icing a bright
yellow and put into a piping bag fitted
with a No. 2 writing nozzle.
17. On the cabin pipe a decoration between each window as in the picture with 3
dots below each one and 2 dots above.
18. Write the name of the boat on each
side of the bow and across the stern.
19. Pipe a continuous line of small loops all
the way round the side of the boat, then
pipe a second line below it but with longer
loops twice the size of the first row. Under
the point of each loop pipe three dots.
20. Pipe one or two yellow lines around
the top of the roof for final decoration.
21. A tiller can be moulded out of fondant
trimmings (any colour) and attached to
the stern of the boat. Alternatively, make a
tiller from cocktail sticks.
22. The railings at the front of the canal
boat are made from pieces of cocktail
sticks painted red, green or black with
food colourings with matching thread
wound around them.

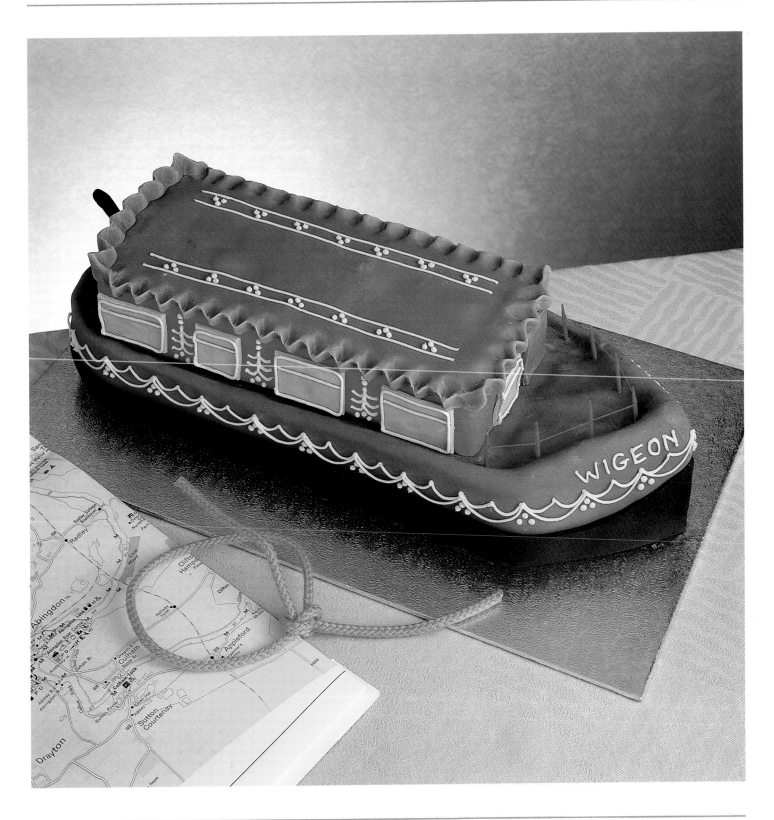

VILLAGE CRICKET

7-egg Quick mix cake (see pages 128-9) or Madeira cake mix (see pages 130-1) or a 28 cm (11 inch) square Rich fruit cake mix (see page 132-3)
6 tablespoons apricot jam, sieved
1 kg (2 lb) marzipan (for fruit cake only; see page 136)
1.25 kg (2¾ lb) Fondant moulding paste (see page 137)
liquid or paste food colourings – green, blue, brown, black, yellow, red, purple
wooden cocktail sticks
½-egg quantity Royal icing (see page 135)

Preparation time: about 4½ hours, plus cooling, setting and drying
Cooking time: 1¼–3½ hours
Oven: 150°C, 300°F, Gas Mark 2; or 160°C, 325°F, Gas Mark 3

1. Grease and line a roasting tin of approx 33 × 28 cm (13 × 11 inch) with greased greaseproof paper or non-stick silicone paper. Double line for a fruit cake.
2. Make up the cake mix and spread evenly into the tin, making sure there is plenty of mixture in the corners.
3. Cook in a preheated oven, tying several thicknesses of brown paper around the outside of the fruit cake tin, and at the lower temperature for 3½–3¾ hours; cook the other types of cakes at the higher temperature for about 1¼–1½ hours or until a skewer inserted in the centre comes out clean. Leave to cool completely.
4. Stand the cake on a cake board of approx 35 cm (14 inch) square. If a fruit cake brush all over with jam and cover with marzipan.
5. Colour 900 g (2 lb) Fondant moulding paste a bright green, removing about 75 g (3 oz) of it before it is too bright. Roll out the larger amount and use to cover the cake completely. Press over the whole cake evenly and trim off around the base.

6. Roll out a small amount of the lighter green fondant and cut into a strip 10 × 2.5 cm (4 × 1 inch). Dampen and lay on the cake centrally, but only about one-third from the front of the cake. This is the wicket.
7. Mix the trimmings from covering the cake and the rest of the lighter green fondant, leaving it still streaky. Use to make 2 rounded trees and 3 or 4 pointed ones and leave to partly dry. Use the rest of the fondant to make a hedge to attach to the back two corners of the cake. Leave to set.
8. Colour 100 g (4 oz) Fondant moulding paste black, roll out and cut out a scoreboard approx 10 cm (4 inch) square. Leave to dry on non-stick silicone paper.
9. Using about 100 g (4 oz) fondant, mould 8 cricketers, each with a head, arms in various positions and legs at angles of running or standing. Give the two batsmen small caps of the same colour, eg. purple, by colouring tiny scraps of fondant suitably; give 5 fielders caps of another colour eg. red; give the umpire a straw coloured hat and also give him black legs and feet. Add a red cricket ball to the hand of the bowler. Using minute amounts of white fondant make batting pads for the wicket keeper and, if possible, for the two batsmen. Put all the figures to dry. Also make two straw-coloured bats.
10. Make 2 sets of wickets and bails from pieces of cocktail stick and stick into the wicket, attaching the bails with tiny dabs of icing.
11. Put the icing into a piping bag fitted with a No. 2 writing nozzle and pipe a 'boundary' line, as in the picture.
12. Next, pipe scores on the scoreboard, as in the picture. When dry, attach the scoreboard to the back of the cake with icing.
13. Pipe *'Congratulations'* on the front of the cake.
14. Using scraps of fondant coloured to

various shades, mould 2 bench seats to put at the back of the cake behind the boundary line to the left of the scoreboard; and mould 6 or 8 deckchairs to add to the other side.
15. Attach the trees to wooden skewers with a little icing and then stick these into the cake behind the hedges.
16. Attach the cricketers and umpire to the 'field' as in the picture, using dabs of icing. Finally, attach the bats to the batsmen. Leave to set.

NOTE: if you are feeling really creative, you can mould out spectators to sit in the deckchairs and on the benches, using about 15 g (½ oz) or a little less fondant for each figure.

AEROPLANE ⊛⊛

5-egg Madeira cake mix (see pages 130-1)
5 tablespoons apricot jam or orange
  marmalade, sieved
4 long wooden skewers
1 kg (2¼ lb) Fondant moulding paste (see
  page 137)
liquid or paste food colourings – yellow,
  black, red and blue
3–4 tablespoons Royal icing (see page 135)

Preparation time: about 4 hours
Cooking time: about 1¼ hours
Oven: 160°C, 325°F, Gas Mark 3

1. Thoroughly grease a cylinder cake tin with lids each end approx 18 cm (7 inch) long and 7.5 cm (3 inch) in diameter with a capacity of approx 900 ml (1½ pints) and put a disc of non-stick silicone paper in each of the lids. Put one lid on and stand the tin up. Also line a rectangular tin approx 28 × 18 × 4 cm (11 × 7 × 1½ inch) with greased greaseproof paper or non-stick silicone paper.
2. Make up the cake mix, either all together or as a 2-egg and then 3-egg mixture. Put the smaller amount into the cylinder tin (or fill to almost ⅔ full) and put the remainder into the other tin, levelling the top and making sure there is plenty of mixture in the corners.
3. Cook in a preheated oven, allowing about an hour for the rectangle and just over an hour for the cylinder. Cool the rectangle briefly in the tin but leave the cylinder for at least 15 minutes before turning out on to a wire tray to cool. Leave to set for 24 hours.
4. For the body of the plane pare off the cylinder cake carefully towards the tail, as in the picture, and stand the cake on a fairly large board.
5. Trim the rectangle cake. From it cut two wings approx. 17 cm (6½ inch) long and 7.5 cm (3 inch) wide at the narrow

wing tip and nearly 10 cm (4 inch) at the other end. From the rest of the cake cut a small piece to complete the body of the plane so it is almost 23 cm (9 inch) long and attach with long skewers right through the cake. Cut a piece for the front of the plane in the shape of a rounded rectangle approx 6.5 cm (2½ inch) square and 4 cm (1½ inch) deep.
6. Brush each piece of cake with jam and keep all separately.
7. Colour about 800 g (1 lb 12 oz) Fondant moulding paste a bright yellow. Roll out pieces and use to cover the main part of the plane, then the wings and finally the front part.
8. Use long skewers and a little Royal icing coloured yellow to attach the wings to the body.
9. Roll out the yellow fondant trimmings to about 5 mm (¼ inch) thick. Cut out a tail of approx. 15 × 4.5 cm (6 × 1¾ inch), sloping the ends slightly, and make a tail piece of approx. 7 cm (2¾ inch) high to fit on the tail, as in the picture. Put them to dry on a non-stick silicone paper for about 48 hours.
10. Meanwhile, colour about 40 g (1½ oz) fondant black and form into two 'wheels'. Attach these to the board in front of the plane and then add the yellow 'front' of the plane, attaching it to the main body with pieces of wooden skewers and icing and resting on the wheels. Leave to dry.
11. Colour 100 g (4 oz) fondant red, roll out and cut into a strip approx 40 × 6.5 cm(16 × 2½ inch), narrowing it off a little at each end. Attach to the plane, over the body and on to the wings, as in the picture, dampening the edges slightly with water so it sticks.
12. Cut out 2 rectangles approx 4 × 2.5 cm (1½ × 1 inch) and attach, one each side of the front of the plane; and then 2 rectangles approx 10 × 2.5 cm (4 × 1 inch)

and attach to the body of the plane just behind the wings.
13. Roll out 25 g (1 oz) white fondant and use to cover the front of the cockpit for the window.
14. Roll out 40–50 g (1½–2 oz) white fondant and cut out a 'propeller' approx 13.5 cm (5½ inch) long with pointed ends; add a small disc of yellow fondant trimmings for the central piece. Put to dry with the tail for 48 hours or so.
15. Colour 50 g (2 oz) fondant a deep blue. Roll out and cut out 6 circles, each approx 2.5 cm (1 inch) in diameter. Attach, two to the red part of the wings and one each side to the red piece on the back of the plane, attaching with water or dabs of icing.
16. Also cut out 19 stars approx 2 cm (¾ inch) in diameter and attach to the plane as follows: one each side on the red on the front of the plane; 3 to each wing between the circles; 1 each side of the blue circle on the sides of the plane; 2 on top of the front of the plane; 3 on top of the cockpit and 2 on the top of the plane near the tail.
17. Finally, attach the propeller to the front of the plane with icing; prop it up until it is firmly set. Attach the tail and then the tail piece to the back of the plane, again attaching with icing and propping in place. Leave to set and dry firmly.

TENNIS RACKET ☺☺☺

6-egg Quick mix cake, any flavour (see pages 128-9) or Madeira cake mix (see pages 130-1) or a 25 cm (10 inch) square Rich fruit cake mix (see pages 132-3)
cocktail sticks
550 g (1¼ lb) marzipan (for fruit cake only; see page 136)
5 tablespoons apricot jam, sieved
800 g (1¾ lb) Fondant moulding paste (see page 137)
liquid or paste food colourings – brown, black and/or blue, red and yellow
½-egg quantity Royal icing (see page 135)
175 g (6 oz) white marzipan or Fondant moulding paste for tennis ball (optional)

Preparation time: about 4 hours, plus cooling, setting and drying
Cooking time: 1–3½ hours
Oven: 150°C, 300°F, Gas Mark 2; or 160°C, 325°F, Gas Mark 3

1. Grease and line a roasting tin of approx 30 × 25 cm (12 × 10 inch). Double line for a fruit cake.
2. Make up the cake mixture and put into the tin. For a fruit cake, tie several thicknesses of brown paper around the sides of the tin.
3. Cook in a preheated oven, allowing about 3¼ hours at the lower temperature for the fruit cake and about an hour at the higher temperature for the other types of cake. Make sure a skewer inserted in the centre comes out clean. Turn the cake out to cool. Leave to set for 24 hours.
4. Draw a pattern for a tennis racket on a piece of paper or card. Make the slightly oval head of the racket about 23 cm (9 inch) long by about 19 cm (7½ inch) wide. The handle should be just over 2.5 cm (1 inch) wide. The main part of the handle should be cut from the trimmings of the cake slightly splaying out at one end for the base of the handle and about 20 cm (8

inches) long. (Together they must fit on to a cake board 45 × 25 cm (18 × 10 inches).
5. Cut out the pattern, place on the cake and cut all around it carefully with a knife. Place on a long rectangular board and attach the handle to the head with jam; use two cocktail sticks to hold it steady.
6. If the cake is fruit, it should be covered now with a layer of marzipan. First cut a strip to reach around the sides and end of the racket, attaching after brushing with jam; then, cut out a piece to fit the head (using the paper pattern) and the handle. Leave to dry for 4–6 days.
7. Colour 550 g (1¼ lb) Fondant moulding paste light 'wood' brown. Roll out and cut out a long strip (or several) of about 4.5 cm (1¾ inch) wide (or the depth of the cake) and to reach from about 12 cm (4½ inch) from the end of the handle round to the same place on the other side – approx 80 cm (32 inch).
8. Brush this strip(s) with jam and press around the edge of the cake.
9. Next, roll out brown fondant and cut out a piece to fit the head of the racket and reach down to the handle as on the sides. Brush with jam, position and press the edges together neatly.
10. Colour 175 g (6 oz) fondant black or dark blue. Trim the edges of the cake corners for the handle then brush with jam. Cut the fondant to a square or rectangle large enough to cover it – approx 12.5 cm (5 inch). Position and then cut out a piece to fit the end of the handle.
11. Mark this handle with the back of a knife as if it has been wound around the handle at a slight angle and about 2 cm (¾ inch) apart.
12. Roll out the trimmings of brown fondant and cut out a second piece to fit over the head of the racket but only 1 cm (½ inch) wide around the edge, attaching by dampening with water.

13. Colour 50 g (2 oz) fondant a deep pink, then divide into quarters. Leave one piece that colour, colour two portions a darker pink/red and the last piece a dark red.
14. Roll out a piece of middle colour fondant and cut out a 'flash' for the front of the handle 10 cm (4 inches) long by 2 cm (¾ inch) wide at the base and pointed at the other end. Dampen and attach to the cake a little way up from the handle.
15. Next roll out black fondant and cut out a piece to fit round the bottom half of the frame of the racket taking it down into a deep point of about 5 cm (2 inch). Attach to the racket.
16. Cut out 'V's of the pink fondant to fit round the black point on the handle and then do the same with another 'V' of the darker red to fit round the pink point.
17. Next, cut small pieces to fit on top of the black around the base of the head, making each a little narrower so the last one tails off to a point.
18. Cut a narrow strip of black fondant approx 5 mm (¼ inch) wide and put a strip around the handle to touch the red flash and then 2 strips on the frame of the racket about 2.5 cm (1 inch) from the end of the coloured design, leaving about 1 cm (½ inch) between them.
19. All round the side of the frame mark slanting lines of aprox 1 cm (½ inch) to represent the strings. Leave the racket for 24 hours to dry.
20. Colour the rest of the icing a pale brown 'string' colour and put into a piping bag fitted with a No. 2 writing nozzle. Pipe a criss-cross of strings in the racket head.
21. Pipe short lines around the side of the frame to represent the strings, in the cuts already made. Leave to dry.
22. Roll 175 g (6 oz) white fondant or white marzipan into a ball and, using the handle of a paint brush, mark the usual markings on the ball.

FISHING BASKET 🐟🐟

5-egg Madeira cake mix (see pages 128-9)
or a 23 cm (9 inch) round Rich fruit cake
(see pages 132-3)
6 tablespoons apricot jam or orange
marmalade, sieved
175 g (6 oz) marzipan (see page 136)
675 g (1½ lb) marzipan (for fruit cake
only)
500 g (1¼ lb) Fondant moulding paste (see
page 137)
liquid or paste food colouring – green,
black, brown and blue
3-egg quantity Royal icing (see page 135)

Preparation time: about 5 hours, plus
cooling and setting
Cooking time: 1¾–3¼ hours
Oven: 150°C, 300°F, Gas Mark 2, or
160°C, 325°F, Gas Mark 3

1. Grease and line a 23 cm (9 inch) round
cake tin with greased greaseproof paper or
non-stick silicone paper. Double line for a
fruit cake.
2. Make up the cake mix and put into the
tin. Tie several thicknesses of brown paper
around the outside of the fruit cake tin.
3. Cook in a preheated oven at the lower
temperature for the fruit cake, allowing
about 3¼ hours, or until a skewer inserted
in the centre comes out clean. Cook the
Madeira cake at the higher temperature
for about 1¼–1½ hours until firm to the
touch and cooked through.
4. Turn out and cool on a wire tray, then
leave to 'set' for 24 hours.
5. Cut the cake in half exactly down
through the centre. Stand one half on top
of the other by sticking the 2 halves together after spreading each side with jam
and putting a thin layer of marzipan in between. Press well together.
6. Stand the cake on a square cake board.
Trim off the back corners of the cake, take
a slight dip out of the sides of the basket,

and then take a slight dip out of the
straight edge of the back of the basket.
Slightly round off the base of the cake so it
goes under a little. Brush the cake all over
with jam.
7. For a fruit cake only, roll out the marzipan thinly and use to cover the cake completely, moulding evenly to fit over the
undulations.
8. Colour 350 g (12 oz) Fondant moulding
paste a mid-brown. Roll out thinly and use
to cover just the top of the cake. Roll out
the remainder and cut out a piece the same
size and shape as the top of the cake for a
lid. Put to dry on non-stick silicone paper.
9. Colour three-quarters of the Royal icing
the same colour as the brown fondant. Put
some into a piping bag fitted with a No. 2
writing nozzle and some into a piping bag
fitted with a basket weave nozzle. Following the directions for basket weave (see
page 48), work the weave all round the
sides of the basket, beginning at the base
and working upwards. Make sure the top
edge is even.
10. Next, work the same weave all over the
basket lid. Leave the lid to dry for at least
48 hours and preferably longer. Leave the
basket itself for 24 hours to dry.
11. Colour the remaining Royal icing a
'string' colour or light brown. Put into a
piping bag fitted with a No. 2 writing nozzle. Work a 'network' design for the fish-
ing net over the side of the basket as in the
picture. Begin by piping slanting lines to
the right round the front of the basket,
stopping it about 2.5 cm (1 inch) from the
base of the basket and leaving 2 – 2.5 cm (1
inch) from the base of the basket and leaving 2 – 2.5 cm (¾–1 inch) between each
line.
12. When the first lines are dry, pipe slanting lines to the left over the first ones.
Leave to dry.
13. Colour about 75 g (3 oz) fondant the

same colour as the piped string and roll
out thinly between the fingers or on a
lightly icing sugared surface. Attach to the
cake around the edge of the basket and put
another strip around the top of the basket
with a small buckle to hold the net to the
basket.
14. Colour 100 g (4 oz) fondant a deep
brown/green, roll out and cut out a strip of
2.5 cm (1 inch) wide to attach as a strap for
the basket.
15. To complete the cake, lay a purchased
chocolate fish on the board just in front of
the basket.

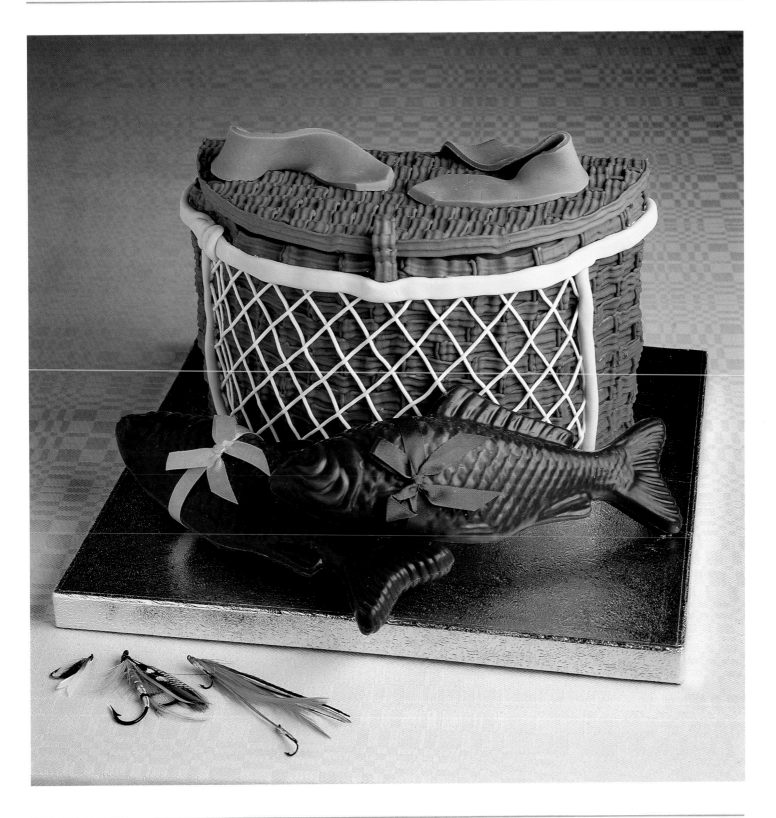

GOLF COURSE ⚐⚐

6-egg *Quick mix cake (see pages 128-9) or Madeira cake mix (see pages 130-1) or a 25 cm (10 inch) square Rich fruit cake mix (see pages 132-3)*

100–175 g (4–6 oz) marzipan (for making hills and undulations; see page 136)

5 tablespoons apricot jam, sieved

675 g (1½ lb) marzipan (for fruit cake only; see page 136)

900 g (2 lb) Fondant moulding paste (see page 137)

liquid or paste food colourings – green, blue, brown, black, red and orange

wooden cocktail sticks

white sticky labels

2 tablespoons Royal icing (see page 135)

1 plain semi-sweet biscuit, finely crumbled

Preparation time: about 4 hours, plus cooling, setting and drying

Cooking time: 1–3½ hours

Oven: 150°C, 300°F, Gas Mark 2; or 160°C, 325°F, Gas Mark 3

1. Grease a roasting tin approx 30 × 25 cm (12 × 10 inch) and line with greased greaseproof paper or non-stick silicone. Double line for a Rich fruit cake.

2. Make up the cake mixture and put into the tin, levelling the top and making sure there is plenty of mixture in the corners.

3. Cook in a preheated oven, using the higher temperature for the Quick mix or Madeira cake, allowing 55–60 minutes and the lower temperature for the Rich fruit cake, after tying several thicknesses of brown paper around the outside of the tin and standing the cake on brown paper in the oven. Allow about 3¼ hours, or until a skewer inserted in the centre of the cake comes out clean.

4. Turn out on to a wire tray, leave to cool and then leave for 24 hours to 'set'.

5. Trim off the top of the cake so it stands flat when turned upside down. Place upside down on a cake board of approx 30 × 35 cm (12 × 14 inch). The golf course can be shaped as you like, it does not have to be exactly the same as this one. Cut out a dip for the pond and attach the cut-out piece of cake upside down for an undulation; also make holes for bunkers.

6. Next, cut a slanting slice from the front of the cake beginning about 5 cm (2 inch) back and taking it right down to the board one end and only halfway the other end. Reverse this piece and stand in front of the cake on the board to make a slope.

7. Using the marzipan, add small hills to the course as you please, attaching with jam. Brush the whole cake and board with jam.

8. If it is a fruit cake roll out the marzipan thinly and use to cover the whole of the cake, making sure it moulds into the undulations. Leave to dry for 4–6 days.

9. Colour 800 g (1¾ lb) Fondant moulding paste a deep grass green. Roll out large enough to cover the whole cake, including the cake board. Carefully position it and mould to the undulations. Trim off neatly around the edge of the cake board. Make 3 smooth patches for the 'greens' and add small patches for the tees.

10. There should be 150–175 g (5–6 oz) green fondant trimmings and these should be made a darker green by adding extra green, brown and black colouring; do not mould in evenly, but leave it streaky.

11. For the trees, colour 6 cocktail sticks or lengths of wooden skewer brown using liquid food colouring and cut into lengths of approx 10 cm (4 inch). Use 15–20 g (½–¾ oz) fondant for each tree and shape 3 slightly taller and slimmer and 3 more rounded. Impale each on a wooden 'trunk' and stick into a potato, to keep them separate and upright. Put in a warm place to dry.

12. Form the remaining green fondant into hedges and attach to the golf course, dampening the icing with water.

13. Make 4 or 5 tiny white golf balls from white fondant, then colour about 25 g (1 oz) of the remaining fondant a bright blue and use a small amount to fill the pond. Use the remainder to shape into a small golfer, not more than 2.5 cm (1 inch) tall and preferably a little smaller. Put on non-stick silicone paper and leave to dry for at least 24 hours in a warm place.

14. Colour about 25 g (1 oz) black, another 25 g (1 oz) red, another orange and another brown. Use the orange to make one figure, the red to make one figure and the top or bottom of another figure and the black to make one figure and complete the half red one. Leave to dry.

15. Use the trimmings of orange fondant to make 5 or 6 golf club and iron bases and attach these to halved or smaller pieces of wooden cocktail sticks for golf clubs. Leave to dry.

16. Use the brown fondant to make 2 golf bags with 3 or 4 pieces of cocktail stick coming out of the end of the bags. Then shape 2 or 3 golf bags on trolleys, again with clubs sticking out.

17. For the flags on the greens stick small pieces of sticky labels around pieces of cocktail sticks, trim to size and write the number of the hole on each.

18. Attach the golfers with their golf bags and trolleys, clubs and golf balls using minute dabs of icing. Add the trees by sticking the 'trunks' into the cake. Fill the bunkers with crushed biscuit.

19. Any message, suited to the occasion, can be written on a space on the cake using the Royal icing.

SKI-ING CAKE 🍮🍮

7-egg Quick mix cake (see page 128-9) or
  Madeira cake mix (see page 130-1)
5 tablespoons apricot jam, sieved
1.5 kg (3 lb) Fondant moulding paste (see
  page 137)
liquid or paste food colourings – green,
  black, orange, red, blue, purple, brown
wooden cocktail sticks and wooden skewers
coloured sticky labels
3 tablespoons Royal icing (see page 135)
icing sugar

Preparation time: about 4 hours, plus
cooling and setting
Cooking time: about 2¼ hours
Oven: 160°C, 325°F, Gas Mark 3

1. Grease and line a roasting tin of approx
30 × 25 cm (12 × 10 inch) and a 450 g (1
lb) loaf tin with greased greaseproof paper
or non-stick silicone paper.
2. Make up the cake mix. Fill the loaf tin to
almost two-thirds full, and put the rest of
the mixture into the large tin, spreading it
out evenly, especially into the corners.
3. Cook in a preheated oven, allowing
about 50–60 minutes for the loaf tin and
1–1¼ hours for the slab cake, until firm to
the touch and a skewer inserted in the
centre comes out clean.
4. Turn out on to a wire tray to cool; then
leave for 24 hours to set.
5. Stand the cake on a round board of
approx 35 cm (14 inch). Stand the loaf cake
upside down at the back on top of the slab
cake. Cut off the right hand corner, placing it in front of the loaf cake. Also cut off
corners and stand some on the cake and
some in front to create hills and spaces for
the ski slopes. Also use about 175 g (6 oz)
fondant paste to create extra 'humps and
bumps' for the ski slope.
6. Roll out 900 g (2 lb) Fondant moulding
paste and use to cover the whole of the
cake and the cake board, pressing it gently

to fit the undulations. Trim off around the
base of the cake board.
7. Use the fondant trimmings to make
extra snowy rocks and attach to the cake
by dampening the base of the rocks with
water.
8. With a finger press out the 'ski run'
from the top of the cake to the base
roughly as in the picture but to suit the ter-
rain you have created on your particular
cake. Leave to dry.
9. Colour about 150 g (5 oz) fondant green
and use to make 8 fir trees. Form into an
elongated sides and then, using kitchen
scissors, snip all over the trees for the
branches. Allow to part set on non-stick
silicone paper and then impale on pieces
of wooden skewers with a little Royal icing
if necessary and leave to set.
10. Colour about 25 g (1 oz) fondant brown
and cut out 6 pairs of skis, about 2.5 cm (1
inch) long by less than 5 mm (¼ inch)
wide. Put to dry.
11. Colour 5 × 20 g (¾ oz) pieces fondant
to bright colours for the skiers. Mould
each to a small person just over 2.5 cm (1
inch) high and put short lengths of cocktail
sticks into their hands for ski sticks. One
skier can have both ski sticks in one hand
as if he is carrying them. Put them all to
dry.
12. Make 5 pairs of flags for the ski run of
red and blue, using small lengths of cocktail sticks and self-sticking coloured labels.
Attach these to the cake each side of the
run at various places. Put the red flag so it
is on the right as the skier comes down the
run with the blue one on the left.
13. Make a 'start' and 'finish' using more
sticky labels and cocktail sticks and attach
this to the cake so it goes over the actual
run and is high enough for the skiers to
pass underneath.
14. Attach the skis and skiers to the cake
with small dabs of icing with 3 figures

going down the ski run, one at the finish
on skis and one standing near the finish
holding his ski sticks in one hand and his
skis over his shoulder.
15. Finally, dust the trees heavily with
icing sugar and attach at various points on
the cake by sticking them into the cake
firmly through the icing. If they are not
too steady add dabs of white Royal icing
around the trunks.

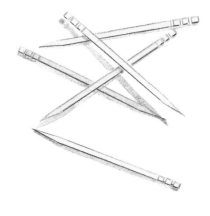

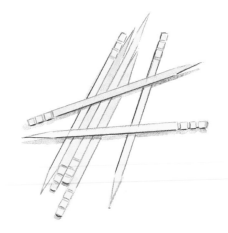

WORD PUZZLE

5-egg Quick mix cake (see pages 128-9) or Madeira cake mix (see pages 130-1) or a 23 cm (9 inch) square Rich fruit cake (see pages 132-3)
550 g (1¼ lb) marzipan (for fruit cake only; see page 136)
4 tablespoons apricot jam, sieved
800 g (1¾ lb) Fondant moulding paste (see page 137)
liquid or paste food colouring – black, red and green
½-egg quantity Royal icing (see page 00)

Preparation time: about 3 hours, plus cooling and setting
Cooking time: 1½–3¾ hours
Oven: 150°C, 300°F, Gas Mark 2; or 160°C, 325°F, Gas Mark 3

1. Grease and line a 23 cm (9 inch) square cake tin with greased greaseproof paper or non-stick silicone paper, using double thickness for the fruit cake.
2. Make up the cake mixture and put into the tin, levelling the top. For the fruit cake tie several thicknesses of brown paper around the outside of the tin.
3. Cook the fruit cake in a preheated oven at the lower temperature, allowing 3½–3¾ hours; cook the Quick mix or Madeira cakes at the higher temperature, allowing about 1½ hours or until firm to the touch and a skewer inserted in the centre comes out clean.
4. Turn out on to a wire tray and leave to cool.
5. If the cake is fruit it needs to be covered with marzipan first, after brushing with jam. Leave to set for 4–6 days.
6. Stand the cake upside down on a cake board, trimming if necessary so it stands evenly. Brush all over with jam.
7. Colour 450 g (1 lb) Fondant moulding paste black. Roll out about three-quarters of it and use to cover the top of the cake.

8. Using a blunt knife, mark the icing into a crossword design of 10 lines each way, leaving a margin of about 1 cm (½ inch) all round the edge. This gives 10 squares down and across.
9. Roll out about 50 g (2 oz) white fondant thinly and cut into strips the width of the 'squares' on the crossword, almost 2 cm (¾ inch). On the top line, beginning at square 3, cover the next 7 squares with white, marking in the actual squares with a blunt knife.
10. Then, add another strip to cover 8 squares downwards under the last one across. Next, put a strip of 4 squares on the third line across to join up with the white square.
11. On the fifth line across put a white strip to cover 4 squares, miss 2 squares and then put a single white square.
12. On the seventh line across put a strip of 4 squares beginning at the 3rd square and then add 2 squares downwards under the last of these.
13. Colour 300 g (10 oz) fondant a deep green, red or purple and roll out to a strip. Trim to the length of the sides of the cake (approx 23 cm/9 inch). Cut strips wide enough to cover the sides of the cake and fold over the top of the cake so it covers the margin around the puzzle. Trim the corners so they join neatly, preferably as a mitre edge.
14. Roll out the black fondant trimmings and cut into strips the length of the sides of the cake but only about 2.5 cm (1 inch) deep. Then, using a 2.5 cm (1 inch) plain round cutter, take semi-circles out of the strip all the way along. Dampen and stick on top of the coloured sides so it touches the cake board. Leave the fondant to set.
15. Colour a little of the icing red and put into a piping bag fitted with a No. 2 writing nozzle. Use to fill in the wording on the puzzle, as in the picture. Other word-

ing can be used instead but it must be worked out carefully before the white squares are added to the puzzle.
16. Pipe 2 or 3 dots on the sides of the cake downwards from the points on the sides of the cake.
17. Transfer the icing to a piping bag fitted with a small star nozzle and pipe a row of stars all round the base of the cake.

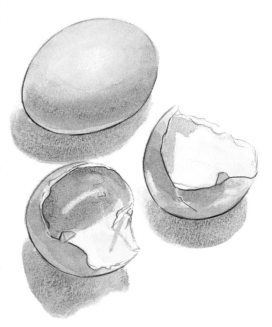

CARD GAME 🂠🂠

5-egg Madeira cake mix (see pages 130-1)
or a 23 cm (9 inch) square Rich fruit cake
mix (see pages 132-3)
4 tablespoons apricot jam, sieved
900 g (2 lb) marzipan (for fruit cake only;
see page 136))
1.4 kg (2¾ lb) Fondant moulding paste (see
page 137)
liquid or paste food colourings – green,
brown, black and red
1-egg quantity Royal icing (see page 135)

Preparation time: about 5 hours, plus
cooling and setting
Cooking time: 1½–3¾ hours
Oven: 150°C, 300°F, Gas Mark 2 or
160°C, 325°F, Gas Mark 3

1. Grease and line a 23 cm (9 inch) square
cake tin with greased greaseproof paper or
non-stick silicone paper. Double line for a
fruit cake.
2. Make up the cake mix, put into the tin,
and level the top, making sure there is
plenty of mixture in the corners. For a
fruit cake tie several thicknesses of brown
paper around the outside of the tin.
3. Cook in a preheated oven, allowing
about 1½ hours for the Madeira cake at the
higher temperature and about 3¾ hours at
the lower temperature for a fruit cake, or
until a skewer inserted in the centre comes
out clean.
4. Turn out on to a wire tray to cool and
then leave to 'set' for 24 hours.
5. For the fruit cake, first brush with jam
and then cover with marzipan. Leave to
dry for 4–6 days.
6. Stand the cake on a cake board and
brush all over with jam. Colour about
225 g (8 oz) Fondant moulding paste a
deep brown (mahogany wood colour).
7. Roll out and cut a strip long enough to
reach around 2 sides of the cake and overlap the top of the cake by 2.5 cm (1 inch)

and also overlap the cake board. Make sure
the edge on top is very straight and mitre
the corner.
8. Colour 550 g (1¼ lb) fondant a dark
baize green, roll out and use to cover the
rest of the cake. Leave for 24 hours to dry.
9. Meanwhile, roll out about 50 g (2 oz)
white fondant and use to make a notebook
of approx 5 × 4 cm (2 × 1½ inch). Make a
ridge at one end and then cut into the side
with a sharp knife all round the side to
make it look like pages of paper. Leave to
dry.
10. Roll out about 175 g (6 oz) fondant
thinly and cut out 7 or 9 playing cards of
7.5 × 4.5 cm (3 × 1¼ inch). Carefully
round the corners on all of them. On 3 or 5
of them mark an edge of 5 mm (¼ inch) all
round. Lay on non-stick silicone paper,
each slightly overlapping its neighbour as
with a hand of cards. Put to dry.
11. Colour about 75 g (3 oz) fondant paste a
bright red and 50 g (2 oz) black. First, roll
out the black fondant and cut out 3 spades
and 4 clubs, using aspic cutters. Attach
these to two of the plain cards as on an
actual playing card.
12. Use the remaining black fondant paste
and the trimmings to roll out and cut out 4
rather larger spades and clubs of just over
2.5 cm (1 inch) to fit on the sides of the
cake.
13. Roll out 50 g (2 oz) of the red fondant
paste and use to cut out 5 or 7 hearts and 6
diamonds, again using aspic cutters.
Attach these to the other plain cards as on
an actual playing card. Then, roll out the
trimmings and cut out 4 larger hearts and
diamonds.
14. Use the remaining red fondant and
trimmings to mould into a short red pencil. Put a tiny tip of black for the lead and
leave to dry. When dry, you could rub
over the wooden part of the pencil tip with
brown liquid food colouring to make it

look more realistic.
15. Colour a small amount of icing black
and pipe the lettering on the spades and
clubs cards. Colour about 4 tablespoons
icing a light red and keep in a covered container. Then colour the remaining icing a
bright red. Use a little in a piping bag fitted with a No. 2 writing nozzle to add the
lettering to the red card.
17. Transfer the red icing to a piping bag
fitted with a small star nozzle and pipe a
row of shells all round the base of the cake;
this may be omitted if the whole of the
cake board has been covered with fondant
paste.
18. Attach one each of heart, diamond,
club and spade to each side of the cake
with dabs of icing.
19. Arrange the face down cards in position on top of the cake and then pipe a lacy
pattern on the backs of each, using the
light red icing and a No. 1 fine writing nozzle, keeping within the rims marked on the
cards. Leave to set.
20. Finally, attach the red and black cards
to the rest of the 'hand' spread out so they
are visible. Also attach the notepad and
pencil to the 'table' with dabs of icing.

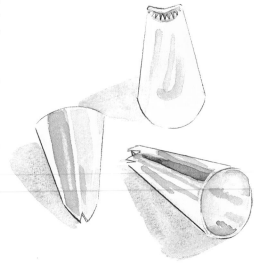

HOMES AND GARDENS

A cottage with roses round the door, a cake with welcome on the mat: the theme of the cakes in this chapter is life at home. From inside the house, choose a sampler or a personal organiser. From out in the garden or greenhouse, decide on a garden pond, complete with waterlilies, or a lovely bowl of hyacinths.

Clockwise from top left: Sampler (see page 76), Potted Plant (see page 74), Rose Cottage (see page 72)

ROSE COTTAGE 🐑🐑

*5-egg Quick mix cake (see pages 128-9) or
Madeira cake mix (see pages 130-1) or a
25 cm (10 inch) Rich fruit cake mix (see
page 132-3)*

*675 g (1½ lb) marzipan (for fruit cake
only; see page 136)*

*1.5 kg (3 lb) Fondant moulding paste (see
page 137)*

*liquid or paste food colourings – pink,
mulberry, brown, purple, blue, green*

½-egg quantity Royal icing (see page 135)

Preparation time: approx 5 hours, plus
setting and drying

Cooking time: 1¼–4½ hours

Oven: 150°C, 300°F, Gas Mark 2; or
160°C, 325°F, Gas Mark 3

1. Grease and line a 25 cm (10 inch) square
cake tin with greased greaseproof paper or
non-stick silicone paper. Double line for a
fruit cake.

2. Make up the cake mix and put into the
cake tin, making a slight dip in the centre
of the fruit cake and wrapping several
thicknesses of brown paper around the
outside of the tin.

3. Cook the fruit cake in the cooler oven
for about 4¼–4½ hours until a skewer
inserted in the centre comes out clean.
Cook the other types of cake at the higher
temperature for 1¼–1½ hours until firm to
the touch.

4. Turn out on to a wire tray to cool and
then leave for 24 hours to set.

5. Trim off the roof by cutting triangles off
the corners of about 6.5 cm (2½ inch).
Brush the cake all over with jam.

6. If a fruit cake, roll out the marzipan and
use to cover the cake completely. Leave to
dry for 4–6 days.

7. Colour 900 g (2 lb) Fondant moulding
paste a pale pink. Roll out and use to cover
the whole cake, apart from the roof. Trim
off neatly all round the base.

8. Divide the pink trimmings into three.
Colour one portion a deeper pink with a
touch of brown; colour another portion a
mauvy-pink, and the last piece a deeper
brownish-mauve.

9. Roll each of the three pieces out thinly
and cut into circles of just over 2.5 cm (1
inch). Arrange these as 'tiles' all over the
roof of the cake, as in the picture, attaching each with a dab of water.

10. Colour about 75 g (3 oz) fondant
brown, roll out and use to cover the board
in front of the house. Colour the trimmings a darker brown and use to cut out a
path. Attach in front of the house and
mark 'bricks' on the path with a knife.

11. Colour 100 g (4 oz) fondant a grass
green. Roll out and use to put a strip of
'grass' each side of the house, attaching to
the board with jam.

12. Colour the rest of the green fondant a
deeper green, roll out and cut out about
100 very tiny green leaves. Mark a vein in
each and put to dry on non-stick paper for
24 hours.

13. Colour 75 g (3 oz) fondant a streaky
blue colour, by not kneading in the colouring completely. Roll out and use to add the
'sky' around the house, attaching to the
board with jam.

14. Colour 50 g (2 oz) fondant a light grey
and 50 g (2 oz) fondant a deep mauve.

15. Roll out the grey fondant and cut into
four windows, as in the picture. Roll out
the mauve fondant and cut out four pairs
of curtains. Attach windows and curtains
to the house by dampening with water.

16. Roll out the mauve trimmings and cut
out a door of approx 7 × 4 cm (2¾ × 1½
inch), attach with water and add a door
knocker and tiny door handle.

17. Mark in the window panes with a knife
and put the cake to dry.

18. Colour 50 g (2 oz) fondant a deep pink
and use to make as many tiny roses and

rosebuds as you can. They should not be
much larger than 1.5-2 cm (⅓–½ inch) and
need only about two or three petals each,
but they must be extremely small or the
roses will look too large on the side of the
house. (See below for moulding roses.) Put
the roses to dry on non-stick silicone paper
for 24 hours or so.

19. Colour the Royal icing a deep brown,
put into a piping bag fitted with a No. 2
writing nozzle and use to pipe the rose tree
stems up each side of the door on the cake,
as in the picture. The roses can climb
where you like, and may go on to the sides
of the house. Add branches to reach over
and around the windows.

20. Arrange the roses, rosebuds and green
leaves on the stems attractively and realistically, attaching each with a minute dab
of icing. Put to dry.

*Making moulded roses from Fondant mould-
ing paste (or marzipan):* 225 g (8 oz) will
make about 30 roses. Roll out the fondant
thinly and cut into circles of 1-2 cm (½-¾
inch) diameter. Taking one circle at a
time, hold at one side and with the fingers
of the other hand carefully press out the
circle until very thin. Roll the first one up
for the centre of the rose and wrap a
second petal around it fairly tightly at the
base but leaving it looser at the top to show
the centre. This makes a bud. Make 2
more petals, each a fraction bigger than
the last, and attach in the same way,
adding a dab of water if necessary to help
it stick. Fold the outer petals outwards
slightly. This will make a medium-size
rose. Continue adding 2 or 3 more petals,
each a fraction larger than the last, to make
a large rose. Rose leaves are made by cutting out leaf shapes from the rolled-out
fondant with a sharp knife and then marking on main and side veins with the same
knife.

POTTED PLANT 🐾🐾🐾

*3-egg Madeira cake mix (see pages 130-1)
or an 18 cm (7 inch) round Rich fruit
cake mix (see pages 132-3)*
*4 tablespoons apricot jam or orange
marmalade, sieved*
*450 g (1 lb) marzipan (for fruit cake only;
see page 136))*
*675 g 1½ lb) Fondant moulding paste (see
page 137)*
*liquid or paste food colourings – pink or
mulberry, blue, green and brown*
*3 wooden skewers and wooden cocktail
sticks*
1-egg quantity Royal icing (see page 135)

Preparation time: about 6 hours, plus
setting and drying
Cooking time: 1¼–2¾ hours
Oven: 150°C, 300°F, Gas Mark 2; or
160°C, 325°F, Gas Mark 3

1. Grease and line an 18 cm (7 inch) round
cake tin with greased greaseproof paper or
non-stick silicone paper. Double line for a
fruit cake.
2. Make up the cake mix, put into the tin
and level the top. Tie several thicknesses
of brown paper around the outside of the
fruit cake.
3. Cook in a preheated oven at the lower
temperature for the fruit cake, allowing
about 2½–2¾ hours or until a skewer
inserted in the centre comes out clean; or
at the higher temperature for the Madeira
cake for about 1¼ hours until firm to the
touch.
4. Turn out on to a wire rack and leave to
cool; then leave to set for 24 hours.
5. Trim off around the base of the cake so
it dips inwards. Brush all over with jam
and attach to a 23 cm (9 inch) round cake
board.
6. If a fruit cake, roll out the marzipan
thinly and use to cover the whole cake.
Leave the cake for 4–6 days to dry.

7. Colour 175 g (6 oz) Fondant moulding
paste a deep brown. Roll out and use to
cover the top of the cake, trimming off
around the edge.
8. Roll out 300 g (10 oz) white fondant to a
strip deep enough to cover the sides of the
cake. Attach, moulding it carefully to the
cake so the base is smaller than the top.
9. Take the white fondant trimmings and
roll out into a narrow strip and cut it about
2–2.5 cm (¾–1 inch) wide and long
enough to reach right round the top of the
bowl. Dampen and attach so it gives the
'bowl' a rounded rim. Leave to dry.
10. Meanwhile, colour 75 g (3 oz) fondant
a deep green, roll out so it is about twice as
thick as usual and cut into hyacinth leaves
of lengths varying from 5–12.5 cm (2–5
inch) and 5 mm–1.5 cm (¼–½ inch) wide,
with a point at one end. Impale a wooden
cocktail stick into each leaf so about ⅓ of it
protrudes from the base. Put on to non-
stick silicone paper and leave to dry for
2–3 days.
11. Take the same green colouring paste or
liquid and use it to brush over 3 rounded
wooden sticks to make the stems of the
flowers. They must be quite thick or the
flowers will collapse. Wipe off any excess
colouring and put to dry on absorbent
kitchen paper for 24–48 hours.
12. Colour the remaining fondant (approx
150 g/5 oz) a deep pink colour or any other
'hyacinth' colour, such as pale pink, cream,
pale yellow, blue or mauve.
13. Take a small piece of pink fondant
about the size of your thumb nail and roll
it into an oval with one end slightly more
bulbous than the other. Take a pair of scissors and cut into the bulbous end just over
⅓ of the way down. Cut each of the halves
into 3 even-sized pieces with the scissors.
14. Using fingers lightly dipped in a mixture of cornflour and icing sugar, press out
each of the petals to a point at the top with

slightly rounded sides. Next, take a pencil
and make a hole in the centre of the hyacinth pip. Bend the petals outwards and
slightly under, and put to dry on non-stick
silicone paper. Make at least 50 of these
pips.
15. Use the trimmings to make 6–9 closed
pips by making the oval a little smaller and
just cutting into the top to give 6 cuts but
not opening them out.
16. To decorate the bowl: colour all but a
tablespoonful or so of the Royal icing a
deep blue and put into a piping bag fitted
with a No. 2 writing nozzle. Pipe a row of
dots all round the bowl just under the
'rim'. Then pipe a zig-zag all round the
side and under every other one pipe two
more 'V's. Put a blue dot at the top of each
side of the 'V's and one at the base of the
lowest 'V' and then pipe 2 more dots below
that. Pipe 2 dots under the single 'V's.
Finally, pipe a slanting line all round the
top of the rim of the bowl. Leave to dry.
17. To assemble: colour the remaining
icing the same colour as the hyacinths. Put
into a piping bag fitted with a No.2 or 3
writing nozzle and use to attach the fondant pips to the wooden stems, putting
about 2 or 3 buds and 12–16 open pips on
each one. They should be attached a few at
a time evenly down the stem and when set
firm, more added again a few at a time. Do
not be tempted to add too many at a time
or they will fall off. Leave to set firmly for
at least 12 hours.
18. When completely set, stick the 3 hyacinths into the bowl, with one at the front
and two behind, attaching with icing, if
necessary, to hold in place. Now stick in
the green leaves all round the flowers,
pushing them in to the cake up to the end
of the cocktail sticks, again attaching with
a dab of icing if necessary.

SAMPLER

6-egg Quick mix cake (see pages 128-9) or Madeira cake mix (see pages 130-1) or a 23 cm (9 inch) square Rich fruit cake mix (see page 132-3)
5 tablespoons apricot jam or orange marmalade, sieved
800 g (1¾ lb) marzipan (for fruit cake only; see page 136)
1 kg (2 lb) Fondant moulding paste (see page 137)
liquid or paste food colourings – cream or yellow, pink, mauve, green and brown
2-egg quantity Royal icing (see page 135)

Preparation time: about 5 hours, plus setting and drying
Cooking time: 1–3½ hours
Oven: 150°C, 300°F, Gas Mark 2, or 160°C, 325°F, Gas Mark 3

1. Grease and line a roasting tin of approx 30 × 25 cm (12 × 10 inch) with greased greaseproof paper or non-stick silicone paper. Double line for a rich fruit cake.
2. Make up the cake mix and put into the tin, making sure there is plenty of mixture in the corners. Tie several thicknesses of brown paper around the outside of the tin for the fruit cake.
3. Cook in a preheated oven at the lower temperature for the fruit cake, allowing about 3 hours or until a skewer inserted in the centre comes out clean; and at the higher temperature for the other types of cake, allowing 1–1¼ hours until well risen and firm to the touch.
4. Turn out on to a wire tray to cool; then leave to set for 24 hours.
5. Stand the cake on a cake board and brush all over with jam. For the fruit cake only, roll out the marzipan and use to cover the cake evenly. Leave for 4–6 days to dry.
6. Colour 450 g (1 lb) Fondant moulding paste a cream colour using a touch of

yellow colouring. Roll out and use to cover the top of the cake, trimming off around the edge.
7. Colour 300 g (10 oz) fondant a dark brown (wood colour). Roll out and use to make a 'frame' for the sampler by covering the sides of the cake and taking it up and about 1.5 cm (½ inch) over the top of the cake. Keep neat edges and trim off around the base of the cake. Leave to set for 24 hours.
8. Meanwhile colour 100 g (4 oz) fondant a rose pink and use to mould about 30 roses and 20 buds of varying sizes (see page 72). Put to dry for 24 hours in a warm place.
9. Colour 50 g (2 oz) fondant a leaf green. Roll out and use to cut out rose leaves. Put to dry over a rolling pin so they take on a slight curve.
10. Make up the icing and colour a quarter of it mauve, another quarter green, a quarter pink and the remainder of it a brown. Put each colour into a piping bag fitted with a No.1 writing nozzle.
11. Mark out on the sampler 'GOD BLESS' on one line, 'AND' on the next line, 'KEEP YOU' on the third line, and 'SAFE' on the fourth line, in the type of print that can be embroidered on samplers. Then, using the mauve or pink icing, work a 'cross-stitch' of small crosses of icing over the letters. Leave to dry.
12. Arrange branches of roses each side of the 'and' with several roses, rosebuds and leaves; make the stems with cross stitches of brown icing. Then arrange a larger spray of roses etc below the 'safe', working the stem in the same way. Attach the roses and leaves with dabs of icing.
13. Next, mark out your name and the date of your birth or any other date on the lower part of the sampler and, using the mauve or pink nozzle (the one not yet used), pipe out these in cross-stitch. Leave to dry completely.

14. Arrange sprays of roses and leaves on brown stems of cross stitch in the two lower corners of the cake and a design of cross stitch in the centre.
15. With the green nozzle pipe a line of cross stitches all round the edge of the sampler just in from the frame on the cream fondant icing.
16. Finally, transfer the brown icing to a piping bag fitted with a small star nozzle and pipe a row of stars or shells all round the base of the cake to give it an attractive base where it joins the board. Leave to set.

NOTE: You can put any message you like on a sampler. Traditionally, the alphabet was also embroidered on a sampler, along with a saying, proverb or a prayer and then the name and date of birth so that in years to come 'granny' could show her children what she had done in her youth.

DOORMAT CAKE 🐾

6-egg Quick mix cake, any flavour (see
  pages 128-9) or a Madeira cake mix (see
  pages 130-1)
4 tablespoons apricot jam, sieved
675 g (1½ lb) marzipan (optional)

Chocolate butter cream:
350 g (12 oz) butter, preferably unsalted
2–3 level tablespoons cocoa powder, sifted
3-4 drops vanilla essence
675 g (1½ lb) icing sugar, sifted
little milk

675 g (1½ lb) Fondant moulding paste (see
  page 137)
liquid or paste food colourings – brown,
  green, yellow, black

Preparation time: about 3 hours, plus
setting and drying
Cooking time: about 1–1¼ hours
Oven: 160°C, 225°F, Gas Mark 3

1. Grease and line a roasting tin of approx
30 × 25 cm (12 × 10 inch) with greased
greaseproof paper or non-stick silicone
paper.
2. Make up the cake mixture and put into
the tin, making sure there is plenty of mixture in the corners.
3. Cook in a preheated oven, allowing
1–1¼ hours for both types of cake, until
firm to the touch and a skewer inserted in
the centre comes out clean. Turn out on to
a wire tray and leave to cool.
4. Stand the cake on a 35 cm (14 inch)
square cake board, preferably upside
down, after levelling the top if necessary.
Brush all over with jam. The cake may be
covered with marzipan, rolled out thinly,
at this stage. Leave it to set for 2-3 days.
5. Colour 175 g (6 oz) Fondant moulding
paste a mid-brown and roll out to an
oblong. Cut to 23 × 10 cm (9 × 4 inch)
and place centrally on top of the cake.

6. Make up the Butter cream by creaming
the butter then gradually beat in the cocoa,
vanilla essence and icing sugar, with sufficient milk to mix to a piping consistency.
Add brown and yellow colouring to give
an icing which almost matches the colour
of the rolled-out fondant paste.
7. Put into a piping bag fitted with a small
star vegetable nozzle. First of all, pipe
stars all over the top of the cake, except for
on the fondant paste.
8. Next pipe upward lines of icing all
round the sides of the cake to match up
with the icing on the top. Leave to set.
9. Colour 350 g (12 oz) fondant paste a
murky green (green wellingtons colour)
using green, yellow, brown and a touch of
black colourings. Halve the paste and
shape each piece into a wellington boot.
Mark a rim around the base of the foot on
the boot with a knife and also mark in the
heel of the boot. A curved line should be
marked on the front of each boot as in the
picture.
10. Use the trimmings of green fondant
paste to make narrow straps and buckles to
fit to each side of the boots. Lay the boots
on non-stick silicone paper with the feet
pointing upwards and against something
solid so they keep in shape whilst they set,
in a warm place for at least 48 hours.
11. Colour the remaining Butter cream a
deep brown and put into a piping bag fitted with a No.3 writing nozzle. Use to
write the word 'WELCOME' on the plain
piece in the centre of the mat.
12. If you like, a cap can be made from fondant and put on to the mat. Colour about
175 g (6 oz) fondant a green colour and use
to shape into a cap (or flat hat) with a peak
and a button in the centre. Put on non-
stick silicone paper to dry. When beginning to firm up pipe a check design on it
with the remaining dark brown butter
cream, transferred to a piping bag fitted

with a No. 2 writing nozzle.
13. When the boots are dry stand them on
the cake, with the cap, if you have made
one, near by.

PERSONAL ORGANISER 👵👵

5-egg and 3-egg Quick mix cake (see pages
  128-9) or Madeira cake mix (see page
  130-1)
6 tablespoons apricot jam or orange
  marmalade, sieved
1.25 kg (2½ lb) Fondant moulding paste
  (see page 137)
liquid or paste food colourings – blue, red,
  yellow, green and black
1-egg quantity Royal icing (see page 135)

Preparation time: about 4½ hours, plus
setting and drying
Cooking time: about 2 hours
Oven: 160°C, 325°F, Gas Mark 3

1. Grease and line a roasting tin of approx.
30 × 25 cm (12 × 10 inch) and a rectangular tin 28 × 18 × 4 cm (11 × 7 × 1½
inch) with greased greaseproof paper or
non-stick silicone paper.
2. Make up the larger cake mixture and
put into the larger tin and the smaller mixture to put into the smaller tin. Spread out
evenly, making sure there is plenty of mixture in the corners.
3. Cook in a preheated oven, allowing just
under an hour for the large cake and about
50 minutes for the smaller one, until well
risen and firm to the touch.
4. Turn out on to a wire tray to cool; then
leave for 24 hours to 'set'.
5. Put the larger cake on to a rectangular
cake board and trim off the corners so they
are slightly rounded. Brush all over with
jam.
6. Colour 675 g (1½ lb) Fondant moulding
paste a deep blue. Roll out and use to cover
the whole cake, trimming it off evenly
around the base.
7. Cut the smaller cake so it fits on to the
righthand side of the larger cake, leaving a
margin of 2 cm (¾ inch) at the top and
base and 4 cm (1½ inch) at the side. Brush
the base of the cake with jam and position

it; then brush over the rest of the cake with
jam.
8. Roll out 225 g (8 oz) white Fondant
moulding paste and use to cover the
'pages' of the organiser. Trim off around
the base and cut into the edges all round to
resemble 'pages'.
9. Roll out 100 g (4 oz) white fondant and
cut to a page the same size as the block of
pages. Lay on the lefthand side of the
organiser. Mark 6 holes in it, 3 at the top
and 3 at the bottom of the page. Do the
same, making holes in the same places on
the righthand pages.
10. Colour 15 g (½ oz) fondant each of the
following colours: red, pink, yellow, green
and black. Roll each out separately and cut
to strips approx 2 cm (¾ inch) wide and
long enough to make 5 pieces to fit down
the righthand side of the 'pages'. Put to
dry.
11. Colour 75 g (3 oz) fondant a pale grey.
Roll out small amounts to make the ring
hinges to fit in the organiser to hold the
pages. Attach and leave to dry.
12. Colour the Royal icing a dark grey. Put
into a piping bag fitted with a No.1 writing
nozzle. First write the words DIARY,
NOTES, REFERENCE, ADDRESSES
and MISC., one on each of the coloured
strips. When dry, carefully attach to the
sides of the 'pages' in appropriate places
with dabs of icing.
13. Roll out the blue trimmings of fondant
and cut out a small rectangle to fit at the
top of the righthand page. Attach and
write PERSONAL ORGANISER on it
with grey icing.
14. Also use the trimmings to cut a piece of
'leather' to attach to the side of the book to
close and clip it shut. Attach.
15. On the righthand page write 'IN THE
EVENT OF LOSS PLEASE RETURN
TO' and under it write NAME with a continuous line across the page; under it write

ADDRESS and 3 lines under it; and below
that TEL: and a continuous line.
16. On the lefthand page write IMPORT-
ANT TELEPHONE NUMBERS and
EMERGENCY 999 and below that pipe
in 4 or 5 straight lines. Below that write
IMPORTANT NOTES and fill the rest of
the space with piped lines.
17. Use the remaining grey fondant to roll
into a long thin cylinder to make a pencil.
Add a tip of black fondant for the lead and
put to dry.

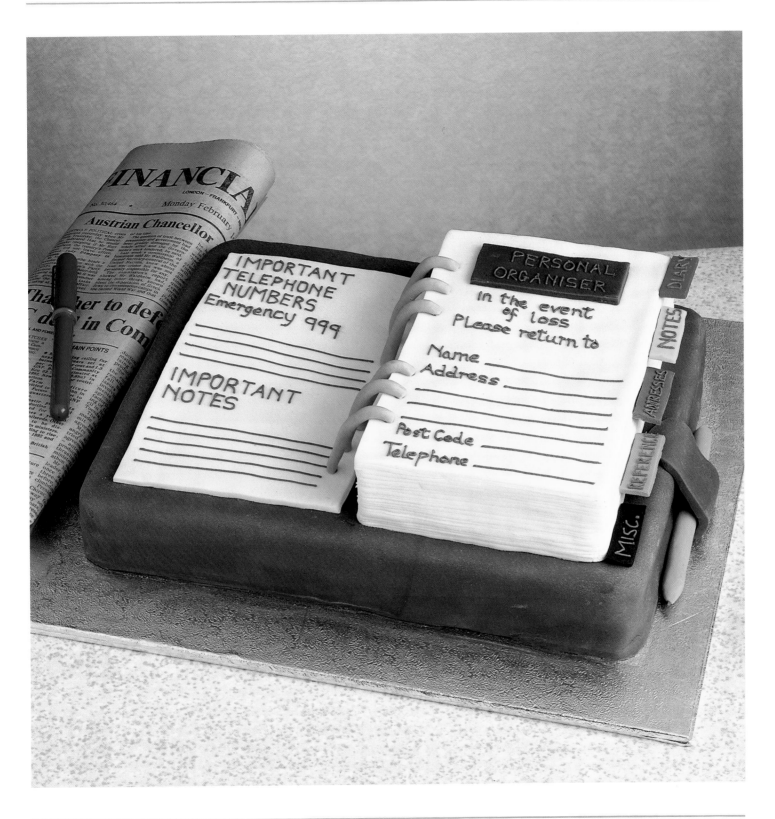

CORDLESS TELEPHONE 👥👥

3 or 4-egg Quick mix cake (see pages 128-9) or Madeira cake mix (see pages 130-1)

6 tablespoons apricot jam or marmalade, sieved

675 g (1½ lb) Fondant moulding paste (see page 137)

liquid or paste food colourings – blue and black

½-egg quantity Royal icing (see page 135)

Preparation time: about 3 hours, plus setting and drying
Cooking time: 45 minutes–1 hour
Oven: 160°C, 325°F, Gas Mark 3

1. Grease and line a rectangular tin 28 × 18 × 4 cm (11 × 7 × 1½ inch) with greased greaseproof paper or non-stick silicone paper.
2. Make up the cake mix, put into the tin and level the top, making sure there is plenty of mixture in the corners.
3. Cook in a preheated oven for about 45 minutes for the 3-egg mix or about an hour for the larger mixture until well risen and firm to the touch. Turn out on to a wire tray to cool; then leave for 24 hours to 'set'.
4. Cut the cake in half lengthwise and stand one piece on top of the other after spreading with jam or marmalade. Stand on a rectangular board of approx 33 × 18 cm (13 × 7 inch). Take a 'dip' of approx 4 cm (1½ inch) in diameter from one end of the slab and also cut off that end so it slopes down about 2.5 cm (1 inch). Cut out 1 cm (½ inch) from the centre 8 cm (3½ inch) of the slab. Brush the cake all over with jam.
5. Colour 350 g (12 oz) Fondant moulding paste a light blue/grey. Roll out and use to cover the whole cake, pressing to fit the curves and cut down the corners so it fits neatly. Trim off carefully around the base

of the cake.
6. Colour 175 g (6 oz) fondant a deeper blue/grey. Roll out and cut a strip 3 cm (1¼ inch) wide and long enough to reach all round the cake. (This can be done in two strips.) Attach by dampening with water so it touches the board and reaches upwards. Make sure the top edge is straight.
7. Next, roll out the darker fondant trimmings and cut out a rectangle 15 × 7.5 cm (6 × 3 inch). Dampen and attach to the cake from the dip to within 1 cm (½ inch) of the straight end.
8. Cut out two 1 cm (½ inch) squares and attach to the straight end of the telephone, one each side.
9. Roll out the lighter fondant trimmings and cut out two strips of 1 cm (½ inch) wide and one of 7.5 cm (3 inch) wide and the other 5 cm (2 inch) wide.
10. Colour 50 g (2 oz) fondant a light grey and roll out. Cut 12 squares of .75 cm (⅓ inch); three rectangles of 2 × 1 cm (¾ × ½ inch); one strip 7.5 × 2 cm (3 × ¾ inch) and one of 7 × 2.5 cm (2½ × 1 inch). Roll trimmings into a 1 cm (½ inch) cube and the rest into an aerial with a knob at the end and a cocktail stick through the centre of it.
11. Attach the aerial at the end with the slope, as in the picture, sticking the cocktail stick into the cake. Put the large grey rectangle on the sloping piece near the aerial.
12. Attach the large strip of grey fondant to the end of the darker piece on top, as in the picture; then attach the longer light blue/grey strip, followed by the 12 squares for the numbers.
13. Attach two of the small grey rectangles at the top of the slope with a gap in the middle, and then the remaining light blue/grey strip, and finally the last grey piece. All are attached by dampening with water.

Use the remaining grey fondant to make a small square knob to attach between the 2 black strips.
14. Colour 25 g (1 oz) fondant black. Cut two small pieces to attach to the slope, as in the picture. Then add the small grey knob between them. Make another tiny black strip to put on to the 'on/off' button. Make a small knob to put between the two grey rectangles and another 2 cm (1 inch) square to fit on the straight end between the dark squares. Make a hole in the centre of this with a skewer. All the positioning of knobs and strips should be checked by looking at the picture.
15. Take a cocktail stick or skewer and mark 16 holes in rows of four, in the dipped piece in the head of the telephone and then make 12 holes in three rows of four at the other end.
16. Put the icing into a piping bag fitted with a No.1 writing nozzle. On the grey strip by the aerial write 'special telephone'.
17. On the grey strip write 'OPERATOR' and '100' and 'EMERGENCY' and '999', keeping the writing as small and neat as possible.
18. On the grey strip write 'RECEIVE' on the left and 'TALK' on the right with symbols in between, as in the picture.
19. Write in the numbers and S and LR on the 12 grey squares and then 'LO' and 'HI' on the two grey rectangles each side of the black knob; and finally 'CANCEL' on the light blue/grey rectangle just below the LO and HI knobs. Leave all to dry.

GARDEN POND 🐸🐸

5-egg Madeira cake mix (see pages 130-1)
or 23 cm (9 inch) square Rich fruit cake
mix (see pages 132-3)
5 tablespoons apricot jam, sieved
1 kg (2 lb) marzipan (for fruit cake only;
see page 136)
1.4 kg (2¾ lb) Fondant moulding paste (see
page 137)
liquid or paste food colourings – green, blue,
yellow, red, brown, black, orange
1-egg quantity Royal icing (see page 135)

Preparation time: about 6 hours, plus
setting and drying
Cooking time: 1½–4 hours
Oven: 150°C, 300°F, Gas Mark 2; or
160°C, 325°F, Gas Mark 3

1. Grease and line a 23 cm (9 inch) square
cake tin with greased greaseproof paper or
non-stick silicone paper. Double line for a
fruit cake.
2. Make up the cake mixture and put into
the tin, making sure there is plenty of mixture in the corners. Tie several thicknesses
of brown paper around the outside of the
fruit cake.
3. Cook in a preheated oven, at the lower
temperature for the fruit cake allowing
approx 3¾ hours, or at the higher temperature for the Madeira cake, both until a
skewer inserted in the centre comes out
clean.
4. Turn out on to a wire rack to cool and
then leave for 24 hours to set.
5. Stand the cake on a 28 cm (11 inch)
square cake board. From the centre of the
cake cut out a 'pond' of just over 1.5 cm (½
inch) deep and to within 2.5 cm (1 inch) of
each side edge and 4 cm (1½ inch) at the
other two edges.
6. Cut off one front corner of the cake and
put it down in front of the cake to make a
slope. Use the rest of the cake trimmings
to build up one side of the cake a little at

the back and to make a few undulations at
the front.
7. Stick all the pieces of cake together with
jam and then to the cake board with jam;
then brush all over with jam.
8. For a fruit cake, roll out the marzipan
thinly and use to cover the cake, pressing
to fit over the dips and dents. Leave to set
for 4–6 days.
9. Colour 1 kg (2 lb) Fondant moulding
paste a good grass green. Roll out and use
to cover the whole of the cake and the cake
board, pressing in to the undulations and
making a split across the pond so it fits
evenly. Trim off around the edge of the
board.
10. Mix the green trimmings with 50 g (2
oz) fondant and colour a deeper green but
slightly streaky. Use to form 2 'poplar'
trees about 6.5 cm (2¾ inch) tall. Use the
rest to make a hedge and add some to the
back left corner and most to the back right
corner, dampening with water to attach.
11. Colour 50 g (2 oz) fondant a deep blue,
roll out and cover the pond evenly.
12. Take 100 g (4 oz) fondant and colour it
a mottled grey/green by adding black,
brown and green colourings. Break off
pieces of this and add them unevenly
around the pond, as in the picture, for
'rocks'. Put some rocks down the front of
the cake and on to the board.
13. Take 25 g (1 oz) fondant, colour it a
dark brown and use it to mould a garden
seat about 4.5 cm (1¾ inch) long. Attach
to the cake behind the pond on the left-
hand side.
14. Colour about 50 g (2 oz) fondant a deep
green. Roll out thinly and cut out 9 circles
of approx 2.5 cm (1 inch) to make into
water lily leaves by making a cut at one
end, marking in a vein, then making 1
small cut each side and pressing out the
leaf slightly to give rounded edges.
Arrange on the pond.

15. With the rest of the dark green fondant
make 3 small frogs. Roll into a fat oval
then cut the head from the feet and lift the
head upwards. Cut the feet in half and add
two tiny pieces of fondant for back legs.
Mark 2 large eyes with cocktail sticks and
put to dry. The frogs should be as small as
you can make.
16. Colour 25 g (1 oz) fondant a deep pink
or red. Roll out thinly and cut out 6 water
lilies, using a small daisy cutter. Bend the
petals upwards and make the flowers look
realistic, some being more open than
others. Attach 2 to the small patch of
leaves and the remainder to the large
patch by dampening with water. Use the
remaining fondant to make tiny flowers to
attach to the piped greenery, as in the picture.
17. Colour about 20 g (¾ oz) fondant a
deep orange/brown and use to mould a
small cat. Take a tiny piece and shape into
a ball, pinching up 2 points for ears and a
pointed nose. Use most of the remainder
to make an oval, split the front of it in half
for 2 legs and sit the head on top. Roll the
remainder into a tail and attach. Put the
cat on the cake.
18. Colour the Royal icing a good grass
green to tone with the fondant grass. Put
into a piping bag fitted with a small star
nozzle and use to pipe patches of 'grass'
around the rocks, pond and over the rest of
the grass on the cake.
19. Put pink 'flowers' on some of the
patches of grass and in the hedge.
20. Attach the trees to wooden skewers
and put into the cake behind the seat,
attaching it with icing.
21. Finally, put the frogs on to rocks, the
lily leaves or on the grass by the pond and
leave the cake to set.

To Mother
With Love

Happy Anniversary

HEARTS AND FLOWERS

Affairs of the heart provide splendid opportunities for displaying the cake decorator's art. What could be more romantic than a wedding bell cake, roses cascading from the top, or a lucky horseshoe adorned with orchids? There is a heart-shaped cake to mark St Valentine's Day, too, and, perfect for birthdays, a wrapped parcel.

Clockwise from top left: Horseshoe Anniversary Cake (25 years) (see page 96), Mother's Day Box of Chocolates (see page 92), Wedding Bell (see page 90)

VALENTINE CAKE 🌸🌸

4-egg *Madeira cake mix (see pages 130-1) or a 20 cm (8 inch) Rich fruit cake mix (see pages 132-3)*
5 tablespoons apricot jam or marmalade, sieved
550 g (1¼ lb) marzipan (for fruit cake only; see page 136)
800 g (1¾ lb) Fondant moulding paste (see page 137)
liquid or paste food colourings – green, pink and mulberry
2-egg quantity Royal icing (see page 135)
few silver leaves (optional)
pink ribbons (optional)

Preparation time: 4–5 hours, plus setting and drying
Cooking time: 1¼–3¼ hours
Oven: 150°C, 300°F, Gas Mark 2; or 160°C, 325°F, Gas Mark 3

If you do not have a heart-shaped cake tin, make this cake in a round-shaped tin and cut it to shape: see pages 126-7 for notes on cutting cakes into shapes.

1. Grease and line a heart-shaped cake tin approx 22 cm (8½ inch) diameter and 7.5 cm (3 inch) deep with greased greaseproof paper or non-stick silicone paper. Double line for a fruit cake.
2. Make up the cake mix and put into the tin, making sure there is plenty of mixture around the sides. Tie several thicknesses of brown paper around the outside of the fruit cake.
3. Cook in a preheated oven at the lower temperature for the fruit cake, allowing about 3¼ hours, and at the higher temperature for the Madeira cake for 1¼–1½ hours, or until a skewer inserted in either of the cakes comes out clean.
4. Cool in the tin for 5–10 minutes then turn out on to a wire tray to cool. Leave to set for 24 hours.

5. Attach the cake to a heart-shaped cake board with icing and brush all over with jam.
6. For the fruit cake only, roll out the marzipan and use to cover the cake completely. Leave for 4–6 days to dry and set.
7. Colour 550 g (1¼ lb) Fondant moulding paste a pretty pale green. Roll out and use to cover the heart cake evenly, pressing evenly over the ridges and into the dips. Trim off neatly around the base and leave for 24 hours to set.
8. Colour 75 g (3 oz) fondant a pale pink and another 75 g (3 oz) a deep pink. Colour 50 g (2 oz) fondant a mid-pink.
9. Roll out some of the pale pink fondant and some of the deep pink fondant and cut out 10 hearts of each colour, approx 2.5–4 cm (1–1½ inch) high. Put to dry on non-stick silicone paper. If preferred, the hearts may be attached to the cake while still soft, but it is much more difficult to keep them in a good shape.
10. Use each of the pink fondant pastes to mould about 6–8 roses, each with 5 or 6 petals and with the petals bent back to give open flowers (see page 72); make a few tighter buds as well. Put to dry with the hearts.
11. Colour the Royal icing a pale and a deep pink to match the roses. Put the deeper pink into a piping bag fitted with a No.1 or 2 writing nozzle and put the other icing into a piping bag fitted with a small star nozzle.
12. On top of the cake mark out and write 'BE MY VALENTINE' and, when dry, overpipe it to make it stand out really well. Leave to dry.
13. Attach pairs of hearts – one light pink and the other dark pink – with dabs of icing evenly all round the sides of the cake, positioned centrally on the sides, and with one overlapping the other.
14. Using the star nozzle, pipe a row of

stars all round the top edge of the cake but just slightly over the edge, leaving a space of one to one-and-a-half stars between each.
15. Take the writing nozzle and pipe loops all round the edging, attaching them to every other star. Leave to dry. Then pipe another row of loops, attaching to the alternate stars, to give an attractive double-looped effect. Leave to dry.
16. Around the base of the cake pipe alternate stars and elongated stars which reach up the side of the cake for about 1.5 cm (½ inch), to attach it to the board.
17. Pipe a row of shallow loops with the writing nozzle, attaching them to the top of each elongated star. When dry, pipe a second row of loops which hang down lower than the first ones. Leave to dry.
18. Arrange sprays of the three colours of roses on top of the cake around the writing, adding the odd silver leaf between them if you like, attaching them all with icing. A further small spray of flowers and leaves can be arranged and attached to the board at the side of the cake. Ribbons may also be attached for extra decorations.

WEDDING BELL

5-egg Madeira cake mix (see pages 130-1) or a 20 cm (8 inch) square Rich fruit cake mix (see pages 132-3)
4 tablespoons apricot jam, sieved
550 g (1¼ lb) marzipan (for fruit cake only; see page 136)
1 kg (2¼ lb) Fondant moulding paste (see page 137)
liquid or paste food colourings: pink and yellow or peach, brown and green (optional)
2-egg quantity Royal icing (see page 135)
1 metre (1 yard) each 2 shades of peach or peach and cream ribbon, approx 2.5 cm (1 inch) wide
2 metres (2 yards) each very narrow ribbons of pale peach, deep peach and cream

Preparation time: about 6 hours, plus setting and drying
Cooking time: 1¼–3¼ hours
Oven: 150°C, 300°F, Gas Mark 2; or 160°C, 325°F, Gas Mark 3

Ideally, this cake is best made in a bell-shaped cake tin of approx 2 litres (3½ pint) capacity or a crinoline skirt mould, which may be bought or hired. Otherwise, make two cakes using 18 and 20 cm (7 and 8 inch) round cake tins, stick them together with jam and then cut out into a bell shape.

1. Thoroughly grease a 2 litre (3½ pint) bell-shaped cake tin of approx 20 cm (8 inch) diameter at the top. Add strips of non-stick silicone paper down the sides and put a disc in the base.
2. Make up the cake mix and put into the cake tin. If a fruit cake tie several thicknesses of brown paper around the outside of the tin.
3. Cook the fruit cake in a preheated oven at the lower temperature, standing the

cake tin on several thicknesses of paper in the oven, for about 3¼ hours or until a skewer inserted in the centre comes out clean. Cook the madeira cake at the higher temperature for about 1¼ hours until firm to the touch, testing as for the fruit cake.
4. Cool in the tin for 10 minutes or so then turn out on to a wire tray and leave to cool. Leave for 24 hours to set.
5. If necessary, trim the base of the cake off evenly and stand on a 25–28 cm (10–11 inch) round cake board, attaching with a dab of icing.
6. If a fruit cake, roll out the marzipan thinly and use to mould evenly all over the cake. Trim off around the base and leave to dry for 4–6 days.
7. Colour 550 g (1¼ lb) Fondant moulding paste a very pale peach colour. Roll out and use to cover the bell completely, moulding carefully to the shape. Trim off neatly around the base.
8. Colour 225 g (8 oz) fondant a deeper peach colour. Roll out and cut a strip 2.5 cm (1 inch) wide. Using a blunt paintbrush handle, roll out the lower ¾ of the strip to make frilling; when it is very thin, it naturally frills as you roll the handle back and forth.
9. Immediately attach the frill to the bell in loops of approx 5 cm (2 inch) all round about 7 cm (2½ inch) from the base of the bell, using dabs of icing to attach. To keep the frill standing out from the cake put rolls of cotton wool under the frills and leave to dry. Remove the cotton wool only when the frill is dry and set.
10. Colour 225 g (8 oz) fondant 2 shades of peach, different from the frilling, and a shade of cream.
11. Use the different coloured fondants to mould large roses and rose buds and a few leaves (see page 72). Put to dry on non-stick silicone paper. You will need about 30 roses.

12. Colour half of the Royal icing a deeper peach than the frilling and put into a piping bag fitted with a No.3 writing nozzle. Use to pipe a row of large dots all round the base of the bell. Above every other dot pipe 2 smaller dots.
13. Transfer the icing to a piping bag with a No.2 writing nozzle and, on the rim of the frilling, pipe a row of small dots all the way round.
14. Next, pipe a series of dots over the point of the frill with a series of 5, 3 and one dot and then 2 smaller dots above these. Leave to dry.
15. Use the roses of varying colours, and leaves if you have made any, to make a spectacular spray from the top of the bell to the base, spreading out as it goes, and attaching each flower and leaf with a dab of icing. (Silver leaves may be used instead of icing ones).
16. Use the ribbons to make pretty bows with flowing tails and attach to the top of the cake with icing.
17. Twists of narrow ribbons can be intertwined with the flowers, if liked. Tie together and attach with icing. Leave to dry and set.

MOTHER'S DAY BOX OF CHOCOLATES 🍬🍬🍬

*18 cm (7 inch) square Rich fruit cake mix
  (see pages 132-3)*
4 tablespoons apricot jam, sieved
450 g (1 lb) marzipan (see page 136)
*about 675 g (1½ lb) Fondant moulding
  paste (see page 137)*
*liquid or paste food colourings – pink,
  mauve and green*
2-egg quantity Royal icing (see page 135)
purchased flower stamens
*1 metre (1 yard) mauve or mauve and silver
  ribbon, approx 2.5 cm (1 inch) wide*
225 g (½ lb) chocolates
brown paper sweet cases

Preparation time: about 4 hours, plus
setting and drying
Cooking time: about 2¾ hours
Oven: 150°C, 300°F, Gas Mark 2

1. Grease and double line an 18 cm (7 inch)
square cake tin with greased greaseproof
paper.
2. Make up the cake mixture, put into the
cake tin and make a slight hollow in the
centre. Tie several thicknesses of brown
paper around the outside of the tin.
3. Cook in a preheated oven, allowing
about 2¾ hours, or until a skewer inserted
in the centres comes out clean.
4. Cool the cake in the tin then turn out
and leave for 24 hours to set.
5. Cut off a 4 cm (1½ inch) slice from one
side of the cake to give a rectangular
shape. Stand the cake on a 23 cm (9 inch)
square cake board. Brush the cake all over
with jam.
6. Roll out the marzipan thinly and use to
cover the cake. Leave to dry for 4 to 6
days.
7. Colour 350 g (12 oz) Fondant moulding
paste a pretty pale pink with just a touch of
mauve in it. Roll out almost half and use to
cover the top of the cake thinly and also
fold up the edge all round the cake to

about 1.5–2 cm (½–¾ inch) high. If necessary, hold this in place with cotton wool;
leave to dry.
8. Roll out the remaining pink fondant
and the trimmings and cut to a lid for the
box of 18 × 13 cm (7 × 5½ inch). Put to
dry on non-stick silicone paper for 36–48
hours until firm.
9. Colour the Royal icing a pale pink, the
same colour as the fondant. Put into piping bags, one fitted with a No.2 writing
nozzle and the other a ribbon weave (basket) nozzle.
10. Work basket weave all round the sides
of the box and also over the lid. First,
beginning at one corner of the box, pipe 3
or more lines using the basket weave nozzle about 2.5 cm (1 inch) long and one
above the other but with a space the width
of the nozzle left between them. Next,
take the writing nozzle and pipe a straight
vertical line down the edge of the horizontal ribbon lines. Then take the basket nozzle again and pipe more lines the same
length as the first ones to fill the gaps but
beginning halfway along those already
piped and covering the straight lines. Pipe
another straight line vertically down the
edge. Continue to build up the basket
weave in this way around the sides of the
box.
11. Colour 350 g (12 oz) Fondant moulding
paste to four colours from cream through
deeper pinks to mauve, roll out and use to
make at least 7 fuschias.
12. Each flower is made from 2 colours.
Using the first colour, cut out 4 petals with
a slightly rounded top and elongated base.
Gently mould the edge of the top of each,
so it is not a sharp cut, then wind the 4
petals round a stamen. Next, cut out 4
sharp-pointed petals from the second
colour. Arrange these round the first circle
of petals, attaching one at a time to give an
open flower.

13. Put each carefully to dry in an egg box
– to help keep its shape – as it is made.
Leave for at least 48 hours to dry.
14. Colour 25 g (1 oz) fondant a deep
green, roll out and cut into leaves. Mark a
main vein and smaller veins in each and
put to dry, over a rolling pin covered with
non-stick silicone paper so they dry in a
curved shape.
15. Colour a little of the remaining pink
icing to a pretty mauve, put into a piping
bag fitted with a No.2 or 3 writing nozzle
and write the words 'To Mother With
Love' on the inside of the lid of the box of
chocolates. When dry, carefully attach the
lid to the back of the box using more icing,
a couple of cocktail sticks to anchor it and
something to prop it in position until it
sets.
16. Fill the box with luxury chocolates,
putting each into brown paper sweet cases.
17. Add a bow of mauve ribbon at one
corner of the box and add a spray of fuschias and leaves sprawling over the side
and down on to the cake board. Attach
each carefully with dabs of icing and leave
to dry.

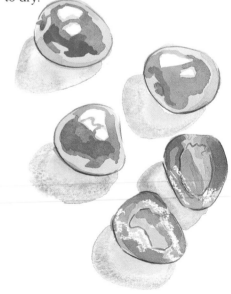

WEDDING ANNIVERSARY BOWL OF FLOWERS

4 or 5-egg Quick mix cake (see pages 128-9) or Madeira cake mix (see pages 130-1)
4 tablespoons apricot jam or orange marmalade, sieved
1.25 kg (2½ lb) Fondant moulding paste (see page 137)
liquid or paste food colourings – mauve, yellow, green, brown and blue
wooden cocktail sticks
purchased stamens for flowers
3 tablespoons Royal icing (see page 135)

Preparation time: 5–6 hours, plus setting and drying
Cooking time: about 1–1¼ hours
Oven: 160°C, 325°F, Gas Mark 3

1. Grease and line a 23 cm (9 inch) round cake tin with greased greaseproof paper or non-stick silicone paper.
2. Make up the cake mix and put into the tin, levelling the top.
3. Cook in a preheated oven for about an hour for the smaller cake mix and about 1¼ hours for the larger cake until well risen and firm to the touch. Turn out on to a wire tray and cool. Leave to set for 24 hours.
4. Cut the centre of the cake out with a sharp knife, using a 12.5 cm (6 inch) round cake tin or bowl as a guide. Make sure the central hole is even.
5. Attach the cake to a round cake board with a little icing and then brush all over with jam or marmalade.
6. Colour 450 g (1 lb) Fondant moulding paste a pale green. Roll out and use to cut out a strip to fit all round the inside of the ring bowl and then put another strip all round the outside. Keep the remainder wrapped in polythene.
7. Colour 175 g (6 oz) fondant a deep brown, roll out and use to cover the top of the cake evenly.

8. Roll the remaining green fondant into two long sausage rolls of approx the thickness of a pencil and add a 'rim' to the bowl on both the inner and outer edges, attaching with dabs of icing.
9. Colour about 75 g (3 oz) fondant deep blue. Roll out thinly and cut into strips 2.5 cm (1 inch) wide. Using a small fluted cutter, take 'semi-circles' out of the strips and place these all round the base of the 'bowl', attaching by dampening slightly. Leave to dry.
10. Meanwhile, colour 100 g (4 oz) fondant a fairly deep mauve; 100 g (4 oz) yellow; and 25 g (1 oz) a much deeper yellow for the centres of the flowers.
11. For the polyanthus buds: take small amounts of fondant about the size of the tip of your little finger; roll into an oval with one end thicker than the other and, using scissors, cut into the fatter end to give 5 equal portions. Do not open up but put to dry on non-stick silicone paper after impaling on a wooden cocktail stick. Make 9–10 pale yellow buds and the same of mauve.
12. For the open flowers take pieces of fondant about the size of the top of your forefinger and shape into an oval with a fatter rounded head at one end. Using scissors, cut evenly into the head to give 5 equal portions. Carefully press out each of these petals thinly between fingers and thumb and shape each to a heart shape, taking a small nick out of the end of each one. Add a small circular piece of deep yellow fondant to the centre of each flower and then stick 3 or 4 stamens right into the centre. Attach the flower carefully to a cocktail stick and put to dry. If it is difficult to attach to the cocktail stick, leave the flower to dry for several hours and then impale on the stick and leave for 24–48 hours to dry completely. Make about 20–24 polyanthus of pale yellow and the same

number of mauve polyanthus.
13. For the leaves, colour the remaining fondant – about 175 g (6 oz) – a leaf green. Roll out and cut to leaves of varying sizes of about 2.5 cm (1 inch) wide and 6–10 cm (2½–4 inch) long. Take a cocktail stick and press into the edge of the leaf all the way round to give the uneven slightly 'frilled' edge of a polyanthus leaf. Mark in the main vein with a sharp knife and then mark in the smaller veins. Make 36–40 leaves.
14. Arrange the leaves whilst they are still wet in six bunches of 6 leaves each evenly around the bowl on the brown 'earth' with dabs of icing and bending them realistically over each edge of the bowl.
15. Attach the polyanthus on their wooden stems by sticking the cocktail sticks in through the leaves of each 'plant' in alternate colours of yellow and mauve, and putting them at different heights, with buds and flowers mixed. Leave to set and dry.

HORSESHOE ANNIVERSARY CAKE (25 YEARS) 🐞🐞

5-egg Madeira cake mix (see pages 130-1)
or a 23 cm (9 inch) round Rich fruit cake
mix (see pages 132-3)
6 tablespoons apricot jam or orange
marmalade, sieved
1 kg (2 lb) marzipan (for fruit cake only;
see page 136)
1.25 kg (2½lb) Fondant moulding paste
(see page 137)
liquid or paste food colourings – yellow,
pink, mauve and mulberry
few purchased stamens for the orchids
pink or red icing pen
2-egg quantity Royal icing (see page 135)
3–4 sprays of fern
12 silver horseshoes, approx 4 cm (1½ inch)

Preparation time: 5–6 hours, plus
setting and drying
Cooking time: 1½–3½ hours
Oven: 150°C, 300°F, Gas Mark 2; or
160°C, 325°F, Gas Mark 3

Horseshoe-shaped cake tins are readily
available, to buy or hire, but if you
should find difficulty, make a 25 or 28
cm (10 or 11 inch) round cake and cut it
to shape (see page 126). Numbers other
than '25' may, of course, be used on this
cake to suit your anniversary.

1. Grease and line a horseshoe cake tin of
approx 28 × 25 cm (11 × 10 inch) in size.
Double line for a fruit cake.
2. Make up the cake mix and put into the
tin. Wrap several thicknesses of brown
paper around the fruit cake.
3. Cook in a preheated oven at the lower
temperature for the fruit cake, allowing
about 3¼–3½ hours; and at the higher
temperature for 1½–1¾ hours for the
Madeira cake, or until a skewer inserted in
the centre of either cake comes out clean.
4. Cool in the tin for about 10 minutes then
turn out carefully on to a wire tray to cool.

Leave to set for 24 hours.
5. Trim the cake off evenly at the base, if
necessary, stand on a cake board and
attach with icing. Brush with jam.
6. If a fruit cake, roll out the marzipan and
use to cover the cake. It is easiest to run a
strip of marzipan all round the inside and
outside sides first and then add the top,
using the cake tin as a pattern. Leave to
dry for 4–6 days.
7. Roll out about 900 g (2 lb) Fondant
moulding paste and cover the whole cake,
covering it as for the marzipan. Trim off
evenly around the base.
8. Immediately take a pair of curved icing
'crimpers' almost 2 cm (¾ inch) wide and
carefully mark a crimped pattern all
around the top edge of the cake. Begin just
below the top edge, covering the joint of
the icing so it disappears. Make sure each
'bite' touches its neighbour and take the
same amount of icing each time so they
are all the same size and thickness. Leave
to dry for 24 hours.
9. For the orchids: colour 75 g (3 oz) of the
remaining fondant a mid-mauve using
mauve and pink or mulberry colourings.
Then colour almost half of this a deeper
mauve. Colour the remainder of the fondant cream by adding a touch of yellow
colouring.
10. For each flower take a piece of deep
mauve and mould it into a narrow tongue
shape about 2.5 cm (1 inch) long and 1 cm
(⅓ inch) wide. Using the pale mauve fondant, press out a circle of approx 3 cm (1¼
inch) with a wide 'lip' at one end. Take 2
stamens, fold in half and lay in the deep
mauve part of the flower. Wind the pale
mauve piece of fondant around it with the
'lip' the opposite side to the 'tongue'. Bend
this over so the edges are thin and keep the
side pieces upstanding. Make sure the stamens do not slip too low in the flower.
11. Use cream fondant to shape 5 petals

each just over 4 cm (1½ inch) long and
almost 2 cm (¾ inch) wide. The tips
should be elongated but slightly rounded.
Put 3 petals together, bending the petals
slightly to look 'real' then put the mauve
part of the flower on these with the dark
mauve tongue touching the cream petals.
Add the last two petals so they come
partly over the top of the flower and then
bend off sideways so they don't completely cover the mauve centre. Bend
them softly. Finally, add a tiny piece of
cream fondant paste to the tip of each
deep mauve 'tongue'. Put to dry for 24–48
hours. Make 8–10 orchids.
12. To complete the orchids take a pink or
red icing pen and draw on a short line and
a few dots to the pale mauve part of the
flower. Leave to dry.
13. Mark out 'HAPPY ANNIVERSARY'
on the top of the cake. Put some white
Royal icing into a piping bag fitted with a
No. 2 writing nozzle and pipe out the
words. When dry overpipe and leave to
dry.
14. On the front of the cake below the writing pipe '25' on the side. Stick silver balls
all over the figures.
15. Put the rest of the icing into a piping
bag fitted with a small star nozzle. Pipe a
row of stars all round the base of the cake
inside the horseshoe and then around the
outside base. Pipe alternate stars and elongated stars which reach about 2 cm (¾
inch) up the side of the cake. Add a silver
ball to each plain star.
16. Attach 6 pairs of silver horseshoes
evenly around the sides of the horseshoe
cake, three each side of the '25', attaching
each with a dab of icing.
17. Finally, attach a spray of 3 orchids and
a few pieces of fern to the top of the cake
each side of the horseshoe with icing; and
add more orchids and fern to the board
below the '25'. Leave to dry.

FATHER'S DAY CAKE 🐾🐾

6-egg Quick mix cake (see pages 128-9) or Madeira cake mix (see pages 130-1) or a 23 cm (9 inch) square Rich fruit cake (see pages 132-3)

5 tablespoons apricot jam or orange marmalade, sieved

675 g (1½ lb) marzipan (for fruit cake only; see page 136)

1 kg (2¼ lb) Fondant moulding paste (see page 137)

liquid or paste food colourings – brown, blue, black and red

1-egg quantity Royal icing (see page 135)

Preparation time: about 4 hours, plus setting and drying

Cooking time: 1–3¼ hours

Oven: 150°C, 300°F, Gas Mark 2; or, 160°C, 325°F, Gas Mark 3

1. Grease and line a rectangular tin approx 30 × 25 cm (12 × 10 inch) with greased grease-proof paper or non-stick silicone paper. Double line for a fruit cake.

2. Make up the cake mix, put into the tin and level the top, making sure there is plenty of mixture in the corners.

3. Cook in a preheated oven at the lower temperature for the fruit cake, allowing about 3–3¼ hours; and at the higher temperature for the other cakes, allowing 1–1¼ hours until firm to the touch and a skewer inserted in the centre comes out clean.

4. Cool in the tin for a few minutes then turn on to a wire tray to cool. Leave for 24 hours to set.

5. Cut out a shallow wedge not more than 2 cm (¾ inch) deep along the top of the length of the cake about 1 cm (⅓ inch) from one edge.

6. Stand the cake on a cake board, attach with icing and brush all over with jam.

7. If a fruit cake, roll out the marzipan thinly and use to cover the cake evenly, pressing into the dip.

8. Colour 675 g (1½ lb) Fondant moulding

paste a mid-brown, leaving it slightly streaky, as with wood grain.

9. Roll out and use to cover the whole of the cake evenly. Trim off around the base.

10. Colour 150 g (5 oz) fondant a deep blue-grey. Roll out and cut out to make the hinges for each side of the table. Cut two rectangles the depth of the cake and approx 20 cm (8 inch) long. Take elongated triangles out of each end of the strips and a dipped 'v' from the top of the rectangles.

11. Attach one piece to each end of the 'work table' by dampening with water or by sticking with icing. Cut 3 small strips the depth of the hinges and about 2 cm (¾ inch) wide for each end; attach one at each end and one in the centre by dampening or sticking on with icing. Mark a pattern on each of the strips; leave to dry.

12. For the tools: colour 225 g (8 oz) fondant a mid- to dark grey and then colour the brown trimmings and the remaining fondant to a deep red or wine colour.

13. Gimlet: make a rounded handle of red fondant approx 5 cm (2 inch) long and add a thin piece of grey fondant for the head about 10–12.5 cm (4–5 inch) long. Attach to the handle with a piece of cocktail stick and put marks on both the handle and head for decoration using a knife. Put to dry on non-stick silicone paper.

14. Pliers: roll the handle out of red fondant about 15 cm (6 inch) long with the ends tapering off and bend in half. Mould the head and teeth out of grey fondant, cutting as necessary with a narrow sharp knife. Attach to the handle and put to dry.

15. Screw-driver: mould red fondant into a handle, as in the picture. Use grey fondant for the screw driver, sticking a wooden skewer or cocktail sticks into the handle and part of the head to keep them together and straight. Decorate the handle with cut marks and put to dry.

16. Hammer: mould red fondant for the handle about 12.5 cm (5 inch) long and 2.5 cm (1 inch) in diameter. Add a piece of grey fondant to the handle of about 6 cm (2½ inch) long and then mould a hammer head of grey. Attach all together with a long wooden skewer right through the hammer handle to the head. Decorate the handle with cut marks and put to dry.

17. Use grey fondant trimmings to mould several small nails or tacks and put to dry. Leave all the tools to dry for 48 hours or until firm enough to move easily.

18. Colour most of the Royal icing a brown to match the brown fondant and put into a piping bag fitted with a small star nozzle. Pipe a row of stars all round the base of the brown fondant (not the blue fondant) of the cake to attach it to the board.

19. Put the remaining white icing into a piping bag fitted with a No. 2 writing nozzle and pipe out the words 'HAPPY FATHER'S DAY' on the top or side of the cake. When dry overpipe and leave again to dry.

20. Finally, lay the tools on top of the work table, attaching with small dabs of icing.

BIRTHDAY PARCEL

4-egg Quick mix cake (see pages 128-9) or Madeira cake mix (see pages 130-1) or 20 cm (8 inch) square Rich fruit cake mix (see pages 132-3)
4 tablespoons apricot jam, sieved
800 g (1¾ lb) marzipan (for fruit cake only; see page 136)
1.25 kg (2½ lb) Fondant moulding paste (see page 137)
liquid or paste food colourings: mauve, yellow and holly green
2 m (2 yards) deep green or cream ribbon, approx 2–2.5 cm (¾–1 inch) wide

Preparation time: about 4 hours, plus setting and drying
Cooking time: 1¼–3½ hours
Oven: 150°C, 300°F, Gas Mark 2; or 160°C, 325°F, Gas Mark 3

1. Grease and line a 20 cm (8 inch) square cake tin with greased greaseproof paper or non-stick silicone paper. Double line for a fruit cake.
2. Make up the cake mix and put into the tin. For the fruit cake make a slight hollow in the centre and tie several thicknesses of brown paper around the outside of the tin.
3. Cook in a preheated oven, at the lower temperature for the fruit cake for about 3½ hours or until a skewer inserted in the centre comes out clean. Cook the other types of cake at the higher temperature for about 1¼ hours or until well risen and firm to the touch.
4. Turn out on to a wire tray to cool and then leave to set for 24 hours.
5. Stand the cake on a 23–25 cm (9–10 inch) square cake board, cutting a little off the top if it is not level. Brush all over with jam.
6. For a fruit cake only, roll out the marzipan and use to cover the whole cake. Leave to dry for 4–6 days.
7. Colour 800 g (1¾ lb) Fondant moulding

paste a light mauve. Roll out and use to cover the whole cake, carefully cutting and joining the corners neatly. Trim off round the base of the cake.
8. Colour 175 g (6 oz) fondant a deep mauve. Roll out and cut into long strips of approx 2 cm (¾ inch) wide. Lay these across the parcel so the strip goes over the top and down the sides as well, attaching with dabs of water and leaving about 4 cm (1½ inch) between each strip.
9. Roll out the deep mauve trimmings and cut out a 'card' of approx 7.5 × 5 cm (3 × 2 inch) and put to dry in a warm place on non-stick silicone paper.
10. Colour 50 g (2 oz) fondant a deep holly green and another 50 g (2 oz) fondant a deep cream or pale green.
11. Roll out the green and cream fondant icings thinly and cut out club or heart shapes using an aspic cutter.
12. Attach these shapes, alternately green and cream, in the wide gaps between the mauve stripes to complete the decoration on the paper. Make sure they are added evenly to keep the pattern correct. Attach each with a dab of water or icing. Leave the cake to dry.
13. Take the ribbon and put it around the parcel as if it were tied all round, attaching with a dab of icing and pushing the ends under the cake.
14. Use the trimmings of ribbon to make a large bow to put on top of the parcel.
15. Colour the icing cream and put into a piping bag fitted with a No.2 writing nozzle. Use to write 'HAPPY BIRTHDAY' on the mauve fondant 'card'. Also pipe a decoration around the edge of the card. Leave to dry.
16. Attach the card to the parcel by the bow at a jaunty angle, attaching with a dab of icing. A finishing touch could be fresh flowers such as a cream rose or two or three fresh fresias by the parcel.

NOTE: The pattern on the 'paper' wrapping the parcel can be any combination of colours and design to suit your taste.

RED LETTER DAYS

Big occasions need memorable cakes, and there are some splendid show-stoppers here. Make the superb Catherine Wheel firework for a Guy Fawkes' Night party, try the bright orange pumpkin for Hallowe'en, or choose from among three colourful cakes to make something special for Christmas.

Clockwise from top left: Hallowe'en Pumpkin (see page 110), Bottle of Champagne (see page 114), Christmas Cracker (see page 106)

CHRISTMAS TREE

6-egg Quick mix cake (see pages 128-9) or
  Madeira cake mix (see pages 130-1)
6 tablespoons apricot jam or orange
  marmalade, sieved
800 g (1¾ lb) Fondant moulding paste (see
  page 137) or marzipan (see page 136)
liquid or paste food colourings – green, red,
  yellow and blue
silver balls
3 tablespoons Royal icing (see page 135) or
  Butter cream (see page 137)
approx ½ metre (18 inch) thin silver ribbon

Preparation time: about 3½ hours, plus
setting and drying
Cooking time: 1–1¼ hours
Oven: 160°C, 325°F, Gas Mark 3

1. Grease and line a rectangular tin approx
30 × 25 cm (12 × 10 inch) with greased
greaseproof paper or non-stick silicone
paper.
2. Make up the cake mix and put into the
tin, making sure there is plenty of mixture
in the corners and levelling the top.
3. Cook in a preheated oven, allowing
about 1–1¼ hours until firm to the touch.
4. Turn out on to a wire tray to cool and
leave to set for 24 hours.
5. Stand the cake on a flat surface and trim
off neatly, if necessary.
6. Draw a Christmas tree pattern on a
piece of A4 paper which is about the same
size as the baked cake. Make the tree the
height of the paper and with three
'branches'. The first should be just over
12.5 cm (5 inch) wide and 7.5 cm (3 inch)
deep; the second 18 cm (7 inch) wide and 8
cm (3¼ inch) deep; and the third about the
whole width of the cake and 8 cm (3¼
inch) deep. Draw a tub for the tree from
the rest of the paper. Cut out to use as a
pattern.
7. Place the pattern on the cake and carefully cut out and around it, using a sharp

knife. Stand the cake on a board and attach
with jam. Then brush all over with jam.
8. From the cake trimmings cut out six
'branches' which are pieces of shaped cake
about 7 cm (2¾ inch) long and 4 cm (1½
inch) at the widest point. Cut off at angles
to give branches, as in the picture. Brush
each piece of cake carefully with jam.
9. Colour 675 g (1½ lb) Fondant moulding
paste or marzipan a deep 'Christmas tree'
green. Roll out most of it and use to cover
the whole of the tree, carefully bending
and moulding it to fit around the branches
on the tree. Trim off neatly around the
base.
10. Roll out the remaining green fondant
and trimmings and use to cover each of
the pieces of cake for the branches; again
trimming off neatly around the base.
Attach to the tree as in the picture, using
jam or Royal icing to adhere. Add one
piece to the top row of the tree; two to the
second row; and three to the third; leave to
dry.
11. Colour about 25 g (1 oz) fondant or
marzipan a bright yellow; 15 g (½ oz) a
deep blue and the remainder bright red.
12. Roll out the red fondant or marzipan
and use some to cover the 'tub' of the tree.
Leave the tree to set.
13. From the red fondant or marzipan
mould 8 bells of about 1–2 cm (½-¾ inch)
long and also cut out 9 small red hearts.
Attach 3 silver balls to each of the hearts
with dabs of icing.
14. From the blue fondant or marzipan roll
out 5 elongated baubles.
15. From the yellow fondant or marzipan
cut out 8 small stars and attach a silver ball
to the centre of each with icing; roll out 6
small yellow balls and also cut out 3 or 4
larger stars for the top of the tree. Stick
these larger stars together with Royal icing
and then attach a silver ball to each point
with icing. Leave all these tree decorations

on non-stick silicone paper for 24 hours to
dry.
16. To decorate the 'tree', first attach the
large star to the top of the tree with icing.
Add the other decorations to the tree as in
the picture, or as you prefer, attaching
each with dabs of icing. Use the remaining
decorations to add to the sides of the cake
which would otherwise look rather bare.
17. Finally, tie the silver ribbon into a
double bow and attach with a dab of icing
to the tub. Leave to dry.

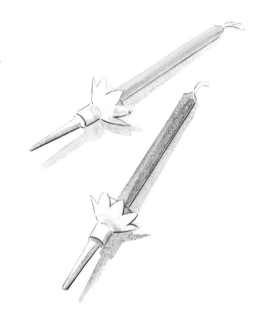

CHRISTMAS CRACKER 🐑🐑

2 × 2-egg Madeira cake mixes (see pages 130-1) or a 20 cm (8 inch) round Rich fruit cake mix (see pages 132-3)
4 tablespoons apricot jam, sieved
550 g (1¼ lb) marzipan (for fruit cake only; see page 136)
900 g (2 lb) Fondant moulding paste (see page 137)
liquid or paste food colourings – red, green and yellow
1½ m (1½ yds) each of white and silver lacy ribbon, approx 2.5–3 cm (1–1¼ inch) wide and deep green ribbon 1.5 cm (½ inch) wide
about 3 tablespoons Royal icing (see page 135)

Preparation time: about 4 hours, plus setting and drying
Cooking time: ¾–2½ hours
Oven: 150°C, 300°F, Gas Mark 2 or 160°C, 325°F, Gas Mark 3

1. Thoroughly grease two special round loaf cake tins of approx 18 cm (7 inch) long and 7.5 cm (3 inch) diameter and capacity of approx 900 ml (1½ pints). Line the lids both ends with discs of non-stick silicone paper. If you only have one tin, make the cakes one at a time.
2. Make up the cake mixture. Put the lid on one end of the tin and stand up in a sandwich tin. Fill to about ⅔ full with cake mixture and put on the other lid. Keep standing upright.
3. Cook in a preheated oven at the lower temperature for the fruit cake, allowing 2–2¼ hours, and at the higher temperature for the Madeira cake for about 45 minutes. Leave the fruit cake in the tin until almost cool then turn out carefully, removing both lids first. Cool the Madeira cake for about 10 minutes before turning out. Leave to set for 24 hours.
4. Cut one of the cakes in half and trim off

just around one edge of each half. Trim off in the same way around both ends of the long cake. Stick the short cakes, one to each end of the long cake with jam and then stick 2 long wooden skewers right through to help hold them in place. Brush the cakes all over with jam.
5. For the fruit cake, roll out the marzipan thinly and first cut a disc to fit each end and then roll out a long rectangle to wrap around the cracker. Leave to set and dry for 4–6 days.
6. Roll out 175 g (6 oz) white Fondant moulding paste and cut out discs to fit the ends of the cracker. Then roll out a narrow strip about 2.5–4 cm (1–1½ inch) wide with a fluted edge. Wrap around the ends of the cracker so it overlaps the end by about 1.5–2 cm (½–¾ inch). Press the other edge flat with the cracker and leave to dry.
7. Use 50 g (2 oz) white fondant to make about 6 or 8 Christmas roses. Mould tiny pieces of fondant into 6 even-sized petals, slightly pointed at the tip and turned up all round. Stick 3 of the petals together and then stick the other 3 together. Finally, put the two bunches of petals together and press together. Trim off the excess fondant from underneath and put to dry on non-stick silicone paper. Press the petals so they curl upwards. Tint the trimmings of fondant a bright yellow. Form it into minute balls and put 6 or 7 in the centre of each rose. Leave to set.
8. Colour 550 g (1¼ lb) fondant a bright red. Form a little of it into about 30 holly berries. Roll out the rest so it is wide enough to wrap completely around the cake (measure the length with a piece of string) and long enough to overlap each end of the cracker. Stand the cake on the fondant and wrap it around completely, sealing together. Press the fondant carefully into the dips at each end of the

cracker. Attach to a rectangular cake board with a dab of icing, with the fondant join underneath.
9. Take a pair of sharp scissors and cut into each end of the cracker to make a frilled edge. Leave to dry.
10. Colour 40 g (1½ oz) fondant a pale green for mistletoe leaves and another 40 g (1½ oz) a deep holly green. Roll out each piece of fondant separately.
11. Cut out mistletoe leaves about 6.5 cm (2½ inch) long with one end rounded and the other tailed off to a point. Mark a single central vein on each leaf. Cut out two sizes of holly leaves, using a holly leaf cutter, and put on to non-stick silicone paper to dry. Put some holly leaves over an oiled wooden spoon handle to curve them.
12. If you don't have a holly leaf cutter, cut the fondant into strips about 2 cm (¾ inch) wide and then 2.5–4 cm (1–1½ inch) long. Using the sharp rounded end of a wide piping nozzle take 'cuts' out each side of the strips of fondant paste to give holly leaves.
13. Colour a little white fondant trimmings a cream colour and use to form a few mistletoe berries. Leave to dry.
14. When the cracker is dry, thread a silver/white ribbon and narrower green one under the dipped pieces of the cracker. Tie each into a pretty bow, trimming off the ends of the ribbons.
15. Arrange Christmas roses, holly leaves and berries, and mistletoe leaves and berries in the centre of the cracker, attaching with icing. Put the remaining flowers and leaves on the cake board. Leave to set.

SANTA'S STOCKING 🐑🐑

4 × 3-egg Madeira cake mix (see pages
130-1) or 1 × 18 cm (7 inch) round cake,
2 × 15 cm (6 inch) round cakes, 1 × 12.5
cm (5 inch) round cake and 1 × 15 cm (6
inch) square cake, all of Rich fruit cake
mixture (see pages 132-3)
8 tablespoons apricot jam or orange
marmalade, sieved
wooden cocktail sticks
3 long wooden skewers
1.4 kg (3 lb) marzipan (for fruit cake only;
see page 136)
1.8 kg (4 lb) Fondant moulding paste (see
page 137)
liquid or paste food colouring – yellow, red
and green
1 metre (1 yard) narrow red ribbon
1½ metres (1½ yards) narrow green ribbon

Preparation time: about 5½ hours
Cooking time: about 3¼–7 hours
Oven: 150°C, 300°F, Gas Mark 2; or,
160°C, 325°F, Gas Mark 3

1. Grease and line the following cake tins
with greased greaseproof paper or non-
stick silicone paper: 18 cm (7 inch) round;
2 × 15 cm (6 inch) round; 12.5 cm (5 inch)
round and 15 cm (6 inch) square. Double
line for fruit cakes.
2. Make up a 3-egg Madeira mix and
divide between a 15 cm (6 inch) cake tin
and the small round tin. Cook at the
higher temperature for about 45-60
minutes until firm.
3. Next, make up a 3-egg mix and put into
the other 15 cm (6 inch) tin; and another
3-egg mix and put into the large tin. Cook
on the same shelf, allowing about 1¼
hours for the larger tin and about an hour
for the smaller one.
4. Finally, make up the last 3-egg mixture,
put into the square tin, level the top and
cook for about an hour until firm.
5. Make up the fruit cakes, two at a time,
wrapping several thicknesses of brown

paper around the outside of the tins and
cook on the same shelf, allowing about 2¾
hours for the 18 cm (7 inch) tin; 2¼ hours
for the middle size tins; and about 2 hours
for the smallest round tin and the square
tin, until a skewer inserted in the centre
comes out clean.
6. When cooked, cool both types of cake
briefly in the tins then turn out on to wire
trays to cool. Leave to set for 24 hours.
7. To assemble: trim the tops of the two 15
cm (6 inch) cakes and stand one on top of
the other, sticking together with jam.
Then stick the largest cake on top. Take a
small semi-circle out of one side of the
small cake and press it to the upright cakes
for the foot of the stocking. Attach with
jam and cocktail sticks.
8. Stick 3 long wooden skewers right down
through the leg of the stocking and attach
the whole thing to a board with icing.
9. Trim off the leg of the stocking by par-
ing away the cake until evenly slanted all
round. Use about 100 g (4 oz) Fondant
moulding paste to mould the foot to the
leg to give a good shape. Cut a scoop out of
the top of the stocking about 2 cm (¾ inch)
deep. Brush all over the cake with jam.
10. If a fruit cake, roll out the marzipan and
use to cover the cake all over thinly. Leave
to dry for 4–6 days.
11. For the presents: cut the square cake
into 3 parcels, one 10 cm (4 inch) square,
and one 10 × 5 cm (4 × 2 inch), leaving
the remainder as a rectangle. Brush each
with jam and, if a fruit cake, cover with
marzipan and leave to set.
12. Colour 750 g (1 lb 10 oz) fondant a
bright yellow. Roll out thinly and wide
enough to cover all of the stocking, apart
from the top and heel. Press to fit evenly,
join neatly up the back and cut out a neat
heel.
13. Roll out the yellow fondant trimmings
and cut a circle about 7.5 cm (3 inch) larger

than the top of the stocking. Attach
centrally, pressing into the hollow and
giving about a 2.5 cm (1 inch) rim all round
the top.
14. Colour 225 g (8 oz) fondant bright
green. Roll out thinly and use to cover the
heel of the stocking.
15. Cut one strip of fondant 2.5 cm (1 inch)
wide and place all round the leg of the
stocking about 5 cm (2 inch) from the top.
Add another strip to lay over the foot,
attaching with a dab of water.
16. Colour 225 g (8 oz) fondant red, cut out
a 2.5 cm (1 inch) strip and attach immediately below the green one on the leg; lay
another one over the foot.
17. Roll out some of the red trimmings and
cut out small hearts approx 1.5 cm (½
inch) across and attach all round the green
strips with alternate hearts upside down.
18. Roll out the green trimmings and cut
out holly leaves approx 4 cm (1½ inch) and
attach at an angle all round the red strips
and on the top yellow band of the stocking.
19. Colour 225 g (8 oz) fondant a pale
green, roll out and use to cover the large
box. Add a few cut-out stars from the red
or yellow fondant trimmings.
20. Colour 150 g (5 oz) fondant pale yellow
and use to cover the middle-size parcel.
Cut out yellow fondant narrow strips from
the trimmings to make stripes on the parcel.
21. Roll out 150 g (5 oz) white fondant and
use to cover the last parcel. Decorate with
yellow fondant crescents. Leave them all
to dry.
22. Tie up the 'parcels' with different
coloured ribbons with a bow on top.
23. Carefully arrange the presents on top
of the stocking as if they are coming out of
it. Attach with icing.

HALLOWE'EN PUMPKIN 👹👹👹

2 × 3-egg Madeira cake mix (see pages 130-1) or a 20 cm (8 inch) square Rich fruit cake mix (see pages 132-3)
1-egg quantity Royal icing (see page 135)
6 tablespoons apricot jam, sieved
550 g (1¼ lb) marzipan (for fruit cake only; see page 136)
1.2 kg (2½ lb) Fondant moulding paste (see page 137)
liquid or paste food colourings – yellow, orange, black and green
wooden cocktail sticks
1 wooden skewer for broomstick

Preparation time: about 5 hours plus setting and drying
Cooking time: 3–5 hours
Oven: 150°C, 300°F, Gas Mark 2; or 160°C, 325°F, Gas Mark 3

The best cake tin to use for this cake is a metal fluted ice cream bombe mould for it will give the cake its ribbed line in the baking. You will need to make two halves to stick together. Otherwise, use a rounded pudding basin and when the halves are stuck together firmly, cut out the ridges down the sides with a knife.

1. Thoroughly grease the ice cream bombe mould or tin, or the basin and put a disc of non-stick silicone paper in the base. Dust lightly with flour.
2. Make up the Madeira cake mixes one at a time and put into the tin, levelling the top. Put half the fruit cake mix into the tin, cover the rest and keep in a cool place whilst cooking the first half.
3. For the fruit cake tie several thicknesses of brown paper around the outside.
4. Cook in a preheated oven at the lower temperature for the fruit cake, allowing about 2¼ hours; or at the higher temperature for the Madeira cake, allowing 1¼–1½ hours, or until a skewer inserted in

the centre comes out clean.
5. Cool in the tin for 10–15 minutes then turn out carefully on to a wire rack to cool. Make the second cake in the same way; then leave them both to 'set' for 24 hours.
6. Trim off the bases of the cakes so they stand flat and then stick together with Royal icing, matching the ridges carefully. Leave to set and stick together completely.
7. If using a plain cake, carefully cut out 'ridges' from 5–6 cm (2–2½ inch) from the top of the cake to the same at the bottom, keeping them 5 cm (2 inch) apart.
8. Brush the cake all over with jam and, if a fruit cake, cover with a thin layer of marzipan, carefully moulding it to the ridges. Leave to dry for 4–6 days.
9. Colour 675 g (1½ lb) Fondant moulding paste a deep orange/yellow colour. Roll out and use to cover the cake completely, moulding to the ridges and keeping it even. Trim off the excess and join it neatly. Stand on a round cake board, attaching with icing and leave to set.
10. Colour about 100 g (4 oz) fondant a much paler yellow/orange and roll out. Use to cut out 2 oval eyes almost 5 cm (2 inch) long; a triangle for a nose and a smiling mouth about 15 cm (6 inch) long and 2.5 cm (1 inch) at its widest. Attach to the pumpkin in the appropriate places with icing and leave to set.
11. From the pale trimmings mould out a broomstick head of about 4 cm (1½ inch) long and cut into it all over with a sharp knife to represent the bristles. Attach with icing to a thick wooden skewer. Then make a much smaller broomstick head in the same way and attach to two-thirds of a wooden cocktail stick. Leave both to dry on non-stick silicone paper.
12. Colour 25 g (1 oz) fondant a bright green; and 325 g (11 oz) fondant black. Roll most of the green into a round ball for the witch's head and mould in a long

pointed nose. Impale on a cocktail stick. Use 50-65 g (2–2½ oz) black fondant to make a lying down cat (see page 141) and add two big round green fondant eyes, and the tips of 2 cocktail sticks for whiskers.
13. Use another 50–65 g (2–2½ oz) black fondant to make a standing up cat. First, mould a head. Roll most of the remainder into a cylinder and cut into both ends to divide for legs. Press these out carefully and push half a cocktail stick into each to keep them upright. Give the cat's back a slight 'arch', putting a pad of cotton wool under it to hold it in place while it sets. Attach the head with a piece of cocktail stick and then roll the trimmings into a tail. Impale on half a cocktail stick to keep it upright and stick into the cat. Add green eyes and whiskers. Leave them to set thoroughly.
14. For the witch, use about 15 g (½ oz) black fondant each to mould into 2 arms with hands. Use about 25–40 g (1–1½ oz) fondant to mould a pointed witch's hat. Then roll out about 50 g (2 oz) fondant for a cloak. Mould the remainder into a triangular-shaped body and stand on non-stick silicone paper. Impale the head on its stick on the body and wrap the 'cloak' around her, trimming where necessary. Attach an arm each side of the body and put the smaller broomstick into one hand.
15. Colour the remaining icing grey and put into a piping bag fitted with a No.2 writing nozzle. Pipe untidy 'hair' all over the green head and down over the shoulders. Attach the hat with icing and leave the witch to dry.
16. To complete: attach the witch to the top of the pumpkin with icing and then arrange the two cats and the large broomstick on the board just in front of the pumpkin face, again attaching with icing. Leave to set.

CATHERINE WHEEL

*5-egg Madeira cake mix (see pages 130-1)
or a 23 cm (9 inch) round Rich fruit cake
(see pages 132-3)*

*6 tablespoons apricot jam or marmalade,
sieved*

*675 g (1½ lb) marzipan (for fruit cake
only; see page 136)*

*1.5 kg (3½ lb) Fondant moulding paste (see
page 137)*

*liquid or paste food colourings – green,
brown, yellow, red, blue and mauve*

5 wooden skewers

1-egg quantity Royal icing (see page 135)

few silver and/or coloured balls (optional)

Preparation time: about 5 hours, plus
setting and drying

Cooking time: 1¼–4 hours

Oven: 150°C, 300°F, Gas Mark 2; or,
160°C, 325°F, Gas Mark 3

1. Grease and line a 23 cm (9 inch) round
cake tin with greased greaseproof paper or
non-stick silicone paper. Double line for a
fruit cake.

2. Make up the cake mix and put into the
cake tin, levelling the top. Tie several
thicknesses of brown paper around the
outside of the tin for the fruit cake.

3. Cook in a preheated oven at the lower
temperature for the fruit cake, allowing
3¾–4 hours; or at the higher temperature
for the Madeira cake, allowing 1¼–1½
hours, or until firm to the touch and a
skewer inserted in the centre comes out
clean.

4. Cool for a few minutes in the tin then
turn out on to a wire tray to cool. Leave to
set for 24 hours.

5. Stand the cake on a round board after
trimming off the the base evenly if necessary. Attach to the board with icing and
then brush all over with jam.

6. For the fruit cake only; roll out the
marzipan thinly and use to cover the cake,

the sides first and then the top. Leave to
dry for 4–6 days.

7. Colour 850 g (1 lb 14 oz) Fondant
moulding paste a bright green. Divide into
five 175 g (6 oz) portions and roll each into
a firework-shape cylinder of approx 20 cm
(8 inch) long with a point at one end and
cut off straight at the other end. Push a
skewer through the length of each 'rocket'.
Put to dry on non-stick silicone paper for
48 hours.

8. Meanwhile, colour 675 g (1½ lb) fondant a light brown with a slight yellow
tinge. Roll out and use to cover the cake
completely and evenly, trimming off
evenly around the base.

9. Roll out the brown trimmings and cut
out a 6 cm (2½ inch) square. Attach to the
centre of the cake.

10. Colour a small piece of fondant dark
brown or black and use to make a large
'nail' to attach to the centre of the piece of
wood in the middle of the Catherine wheel
to hold it on to the post. Leave to dry.

11. Colour 25 g (1 oz) fondant a dark blue/
mauve for the 'touch paper'. Mould into 5
pieces for the 'touch paper', pressing out
the ends of it thinly, and attach to the ends
of the fireworks with icing.

12. Colour 50 g (2 oz) fondant red; roll out
thinly and use to cover the tips of each of
the fireworks, attaching it by dampening
with water.

13. Colour 25 g (1 oz) fondant bright
yellow and another 25 g (1 oz) bright
orange. Roll out both pieces thinly.

14. Cut 10 narrow strips from the yellow
fondant about 1.5 cm (½ inch) wide. Wind
around the fireworks, keeping them in
equi-distant bands on each one.

15. Cut out tiny stars from the orange fondant about 1.5 cm (½ inch) wide. Attach all
over the green parts of the fireworks,
either by dampening with water or attach
with small dabs of icing. Leave to dry.

16. Colour the Royal icing a pale brown to
match the fondant-covered cake and put
into a piping bag fitted with a star nozzle.
Pipe a border of stars all around the base of
the cake with two stars above every alternate star. A border of stars could also be
piped around the top edge of the cake if
you like. (The stars, either every one or
every other one, could be decorated with
coloured balls.) Leave to set.

17. Arrange the five fireworks evenly on
top of the cake so they are at an angle on
the cake and protrude over the edge, as in
the picture. Attach with icing. Roll out
small sausage shapes of the remaining
white fondant of approx 1 cm (⅓ inch) in
diameter and cut lengths to attach the
head of one firework on the cake to the tail
of the next: in theory, when lit the fuse of
white would light all the fireworks and
make them revolve as a Catherine wheel
does. Finally, add a tiny piece of white fuse
sticking outwards and put a small 'blue
touch paper' to the end of it ready for
lighting.

BOTTLE OF CHAMPAGNE

2 × 2-egg Madeira cake mix (see pages 130-1) or an 18 cm (7 inch) round Rich fruit cake mix (see pages 132-3)
3 long wooden skewers
6 tablespoons apricot jam, sieved
350 g (12 oz) marzipan (see page 136)
850 g (1 lb 14 oz) Fondant moulding paste (see page 137)
liquid or paste food colourings – green, black, red and yellow
1-egg quantity Royal icing (see page 135)

Preparation time: about 3½ hours, plus setting and drying
Cooking time: 1–2¼ hours
Oven: 150°C, 300°F, Gas Mark 2; or, 160°C, 325°F, Gas Mark 3

It is quite difficult to achieve the correct shape for a bottle from cake, but either use a special cylindrical cake tin with lids each end; or bake 3 or 4 12.4 cm (5 inch) round cakes and when set trim off the tops and stick together. You would have to add marzipan to the lower part of the cake if using the cylindrical tin to achieve the extra width which differentiates a champagne bottle from an ordinary wine bottle.

1. Thoroughly grease a cylindrical cake tin with lids both ends of approx 8 cm (3¼ inch) diameter and 16.5 cm (6¾ inch) long. Grease the lids and put in a disc of non-stick silicone paper. Put the lid on one end of the tin and stand up. For fruit cake it is best to line with greased greaseproof paper or non-stick paper if possible, but it is a little tricky.
2. Make up a 2-egg Madeira cake mix and put into the tin or make up the fruit cake mixture and put about half of it to come ⅔ of the way up the tin. Put the other lid on the top. Wrap sheets of brown paper around the outside of the tin for the fruit cake.

3. Cook in a preheated oven at the lower temperature for the fruit cake, allowing about 2¼ hours; or for about 1 hour at the higher temperature for the Madeira cake.
4. Leave the fruit cake to cool for 30–40 minutes or the Madeira cake for 15 minutes in the tin before turning out carefully on to a wire tray to cool.
5. Wash, dry and regrease and/or reline the tin and either put in the remainder of the fruit cake mixture or make up the second Madeira mixture and put into the tin. Cook and cool as before.
6. When cold leave to set for 24 hours.
7. Trim off the base and tops of the cakes evenly and stick together with icing. Push 3 long skewers right through the cake from top to base, keeping them close together and central in the cake because of the narrow neck to be shaped.
8. If possible, have a champagne or sparkling wine bottle available to show the slightly bulbous shape of the bottle, or copy the picture. With a narrow serrated knife carefully pare away the top of the cake to give the neck of the bottle and where it splays out. Keep the neck central and straight and make it thicker at first; you can always pare off more if necessary.
9. Stand the cake (or bottle as it now is) on a small round cake board and attach with icing. Leave to dry then brush all over with jam.
10. For both types of cake roll out the marzipan thinly and use to cover the whole of the bottle for the fruit cake, but very thinly up the neck; and just up to the beginning of the shaping for the Madeira cake. Press it evenly to prevent a ridge.
11. Colour 550 g (1¼ lb) Fondant moulding paste a deep 'bottle' green using both green and a touch of black. Roll out and use to cover the bottle up to about 5 cm (2 inch) up the neck of the bottle. Trim off the fondant neatly around the base and

press the top edge to the cake.
12. Colour 175 g (6 oz) fondant black. Roll out some of it and cut a label of approx 11 × 7.5 cm (4½ × 3 inch). Dampen the edges and attach the label to the front of the bottle. Leave to dry.
13. Roll out the remainder thinly and use to cover the head and most of the neck of the bottle to join the green fondant and dipping down to a 'v' at the front. Cut a strip and put around the neck of the bottle, then roll out the black fondant trimmings and put a 'top' on the bottle. Cover the rim and finish the top with a small twisted point.
14. Colour 65 g (2½ oz) fondant red and 40 g (1½ oz) a deep yellow.
15. Roll out the red fondant and cut out a strip approx 1.5 cm (½ inch) wide and put around the neck of the bottle for a flash. Attach to the cake.
16. Cut out a strip of red to go round the edge of the black 'v' on the bottle about 2 cm (¾ inch) wide and attach by dampening with water. Cut out a round fluted disc 2.5 cm (1 inch) across.
17. Roll out the yellow fondant and cut out a narrow strip to fit under the red strip, descending into a 'v'; attach. Also cut a 2 cm (¾ inch) plain disc.
18. Attach the red disc to the dipped 'v' and put the yellow disc centrally on top.
19. Put the Royal icing into a piping bag fitted with a No. 1 writing nozzle and on the red flash pipe 'BRUT'; on the red 'V' write the name 'CHARLES' or a name suited to the occasion.
20. On the label first write 'CHAMPAGNE' at the top with a few lines around it. Below write 'CHARLES & SON' and centrally at the bottom write '75 cl'.
21. Finally, pipe a decoration on the yellow disc and leave to set.

NEWSPAPER

4-egg Madeira cake mix (see pages 130-1) or an 18 cm (7 inch) square Rich fruit cake mix (see pages 132-3)
6 tablespoons apricot jam or orange marmalade
550 g (1¼ lb) marzipan (for fruit cake only; see page 136)
900 g (2 lb) Fondant moulding paste (see page 136)
1-egg quantity Royal icing (see page 135)
liquid or paste food colourings – black and red

Preparation time: about 4 hours, plus cooling, drying and setting
Cooking time: 1¼–3 hours
Oven: 150°C, 300°F, Gas Mark 2; or 160°C, 325°F, Gas Mark 3

1. Grease and line a rectangular tin approx 28 × 18 × 4 cm (11 × 7 × 1½ inch) with greased greaseproof paper or non-stick silicone paper. Double line for a fruit cake.
2. Make up the cake mix and put into the tin, levelling the top and making sure there is plenty of mixture in the corners. Tie several thicknesses of brown paper around the outside of the tin for a fruit cake.
3. Cook in a preheated oven at the lower temperature and standing on several layers of brown paper for the fruit cake, allowing 2¼–3 hours until a skewer inserted in the centre comes out clean; and at the higher temperature for the Madeira cake, allowing 1–1¼ hours until firm to the touch.
4. Cool the Madeira cake briefly in the tin before turning out but leave the fruit cake for longer and preferably until quite cool before turning out on to a wire tray to cool completely. Leave to set for 24 hours.
5. Mark a line across the length of the centre of the cake and cut off a thin slanting slice from this line to the edge of the

cake. Turn it upside down and invert on to the other half of the cake to give a slanting cake; attach with jam or marmalade.
6. Sieve the remaining jam and use to brush all over the cake. Stand the cake on a cakeboard.
7. For a fruit cake only, roll out the marzipan thinly and use to cover the cake evenly, putting pieces on the end first, and then laying a wide strip over the rest of the cake. Trim and leave to dry for 4–6 days.
8. Roll out 350 g (¾ lb) Fondant moulding paste and use to cover all round the side of the cake, slightly overlapping on to the top. Trim off around the base.
9. Roll out the remaining fondant and trimmings rather thicker than usual and trim to a rectangle approx 28 × 35 cm (11 × 14 inch), long enough to cover the top of the cake and fold back over for the pages.
10. Attach the fondant, beginning at the front and taking it over to the back. Lay a rolled-up piece of kitchen paper along the length of the cake at the back and fold the fondant strip over the paper to give it a curve, as in the picture, to represent a newspaper with a fold. Mark a slightly 'wavy edge' along the top edge of the icing as on a normal newspaper.
11. Mark cuts into the fondant on the left-hand side and front of the cake, taking care not to cut it right through, to represent the pages. Leave to set for 24 hours.
12. Colour most of the Royal icing black and put into a piping bag fitted with a No. 1 or No. 0 writing nozzle.
13. Mark the newspaper into 'columns', as in the picture, and put a heading at the top saying either PERSONAL or ANNOUN-CEMENTS; then write BIRTHS and MARRIAGES in appropriate places.
14. Decide what you are going to write on the newspaper and then put in 'pretend adverts' by piping 'squiggle words', as in the picture. Carefully write in your chosen

advert, keeping the writing as small and neat as possible but still clear and readable. It should be placed fairly centrally.
15. Fill in any 'writing' necessary on the under page of the newspaper, again in squiggle writing, to make it look authentic and then leave all to dry.
16. Finally, colour the remaining icing bright red and put into a piping bag fitted with a No. 1 or No. 2 writing nozzle. Pipe a circle around your advertisement to make it stand out and leave to dry.
17. Very carefully remove the piece of kitchen paper holding the icing up to dry and the cake is complete.

EXAM SUCCESS

2 × 3-egg Madeira cake mixes (see pages 130-1) or 1 × 15 cm (6 inch) square and 1 × 18 cm (7 inch) square Rich fruit cake mixes (see pages 132-3)

6 tablespoons apricot jam or orange marmalade, sieved

800 g (1¾ lb) marzipan (for fruit cake only; see page 136)

1 kg (2¼ lb) Fondant moulding paste (see page 137)

liquid or paste food colourings – blue, green and yellow

2-egg quantity Royal icing (see page 135)

1½ metres (1½ yards) each royal blue, green or deep turquoise/green ribbon 2.5 cm (1 inch) wide

1 metre (1 yard) each royal blue and green or turquoise/green ribbon 1.5 cm (½ inch) wide

silver or blue or green balls

Preparation time: about 4 hours
Cooking time: 1–2¾ hours
Oven: 150°C, 300°F, Gas Mark 2; or, 160°C, 325°F, Gas Mark 3

1. Grease and line two rectangular tins 28 × 18 × 4 cm (11 × 7 × 1½ inch) with greased greaseproof paper or non-stick silicone paper. Double line for a fruit cake.
2. Make up the cake mixes separately for the Madeira cake and together for the fruit cake and put into the tins, levelling the tops and making sure there is plenty of mixture in the corners.
3. Tie several thicknesses of brown paper around the outside of the fruit cakes. Cook in a preheated oven at the lower temperature for the fruit cake for about 2¾ hours until a skewer inserted in the centre comes out clean; and at the higher temperature for the other cakes, allowing 50-60 mins until well risen and firm to the touch. They should both be baked on the same shelf.

4. Cool the fruit cakes completely in the tin or Madeira for about 10 minutes before turning out on wire trays to cool. Leave to set for 24 hours.
5. Level the tops of the cakes, if necessary, then cut off a 5 cm (2 inch) slice from the length of one of the cakes.
6. Stand the larger cake on a board and attach with Royal icing. Brush the top with jam and place the smaller cake on top so the backs are level and there is a step down on the front of the cake. Brush with jam all over.
7. For the fruit cake only, roll out the marzipan thinly and cover the cake completely by covering the ends first and then laying a wide strip to cover the rest of the cake from the back to the front. Trim off evenly. Leave to dry for 4-6 days.
8. Colour 765 g (1½ lb) Fondant moulding paste a pale blue. Roll out and use to cover the whole cake evenly, moulding to the undulations and cover the corners neatly. Trim off around the base and leave to dry for 24 hours.
9. Colour 175 g (6 oz) fondant a pale yellow or parchment colour by adding a touch of yellow colouring, roll out and cut to a rectangle of approx 20 × 15 cm (8 × 6 inch). Roll up loosely to make a scroll and press out the edge of the fondant thinly to make it look like paper. Put to dry on non-stick silicone paper for 48 hours.
10. Colour the pale blue fondant trimmings a much deeper blue, roll out and use to cut out six 'glasses' about 3 cm (1¼ inch) high. Attach to the sides of the cake, two at the back end and one on the side of the narrow part.
11. Also cut out a disc approx 4 cm (1½ inch) in diameter from the deep blue fondant and then a small blue star.
12. Colour a tiny piece of the yellow fondant a much deeper yellow, roll out and use to cut a 2.5 cm (1 inch) fluted disc.

Attach this centrally to the blue circle and put the blue star on top, attaching with a dab of water or icing. Leave to set.
13. Lay a piece of wide green ribbon across the cake from the back to the front, as in the picture, in a 'V' and then put a narrow strip of blue or turquois/green on top. Attach at the back and at the front with icing. Next, attach the blue and yellow 'medal' at the point of the ribbon with icing.
14. Tie the 'scroll' up with a narrow or wide green or blue ribbon, or both, adding a bow. Attach to the back of the cake with icing between the 'V' of ribbons.
15. Colour the icing a deep blue or green to contrast with the pale blue fondant covering. Put some into a piping bag fitted with a No. 2 writing nozzle and pipe out the word CONGRATULATIONS just in front of the scroll. When dry overpipe.
16. On the sides of the cake between the cut-out glasses write NO MORE EXAMS!
17. Put some icing into a piping bag fitted with a star nozzle and pipe a row of stars and elongated stars all round the base of the cake.
18. Also, pipe a row of stars along the top back edge of the cake and down the back corners.
19. Take the writing nozzle and pipe loops all round the base of the cake, attaching each to the top of the elongated stars.
20. Pipe a row of loops along the top edge on the side of the cake and along the front edge but stopping where the ribbon falls. Then pipe a second row of loops in between the first ones, dropping them a little lower. Do the same on the lower edge and front edge of the cake.
21. Complete the icing decoration by piping dots with the writing nozzle, as in the picture. Leave to dry.

EASTER CHICK

5-egg Quick mix cake (see pages 128-9) or
Madeira cake mix (see pages 130-1)
4 tablespoons apricot jam or marmalade,
sieved
550 g (1¼ lb) Fondant moulding paste (see
pages 137)
liquid or paste food colourings – orange,
yellow, blue, green and black

Butter cream:
350 g (12 oz) unsalted butter
675 g (1½ lb) icing sugar, sifted
1–2 tablespoons lemon juice

Preparation time: about 3½–4 hours,
plus setting and drying
Cooking time: about 2½ hours
Oven: 160°C, 325°F, Gas Mark 3

1. Thoroughly grease a round oven proof
bowl of approx 2 litres (3½ pints) capacity
and 20–22 cm (8–8½ inch) diameter and a
basin of 600–900 ml (1–1½ pints). Put a
disc of non-stick silicone paper in the base
of each basin and lightly dredge the sides
with flour.
2. Make up the cake mix and divide between the two bowls, filling them so they
are filled to the same level. Make sure the
tops are level and not humped up in the
middle.
3. Cook in a preheated oven, allowing
about 50 minutes for the small cake and
about 1½ hours for the large one, until well
risen and firm, and a skewer inserted in
the centre comes out clean. It may be
necessary to cook the cakes one at a time to
get them evenly cooked.
4. Cool in the basins for 5 minutes then
turn out carefully on to wire trays to cool;
peel off the paper discs. Leave to set for 24
hours.
5. Trim off the base of the cakes evenly.
Stand the large cake on a square cake
board for the body. Take out a small semi-

circle from towards the top and add the
smaller cake for the head, attaching with
jam. Brush all over both cakes with jam.
6. Colour 100 g (4 oz) Fondant moulding
paste a bright orange colour and use part
of it to mould a pointed beak. Attach to
the front of the head in the appropriate
place with jam. Wrap the remaining
orange fondant in polythene.
7. Colour about 175 g (6 oz) fondant a
bright sky blue, leaving it a little streaky, if
preferred. Roll out thinly and attach to the
upper part of the board all around the
chick to represent the sky, after brushing
the board with jam. A couple of clouds
may be added; make them by rolling out
small pieces of white fondant, cutting
them to cloud shapes and attaching to the
blue fondant by simply dampening
lightly.
8. Colour 225 g (8 oz) fondant a grass
green; roll out thinly and use to cover the
lower part of the board, around the chick
and to meet the 'sky', again after brushing
the board with jam. Leave to set.
9. Roll out the remaining orange fondant
and use to mould two long legs with claw-
like feet for the chick. Attach to the board
and the body, by dampening slightly.
10. Make up the Butter cream by creaming
the butter until soft then gradually beating
in the icing sugar and lemon juice to give a
piping consistency. Add yellow colouring
to give a typical 'chick' yellow colour.
11. Put most of the Butter cream into a piping bag fitted with a small star vegetable
nozzle. Pipe elongated upright stars or
squiggles all over the head and body of the
chick to represent feathers and then pipe a
few long streaks of icing to make 'tail
feathers'.
12. Colour the remaining Butter cream a
grass green and put into a piping bag fitted
with a small star nozzle (not a vegetable
nozzle). Pipe out squiggles of Butter cream

all over the 'grass' with some longer
patches for 'rough grass'.
13. Colour a tiny piece of fondant trimmings black and add to the chick for an
eye. Leave to set.

CAKES FOR OCCASIONS

$\mathcal{F}$OOD FACTS

HELEN DORE

MAKING NOVELTY CAKES

An imaginative, beautifully decorated novelty cake makes any party occasion really special, whether it's a child's christening or birthday, an engagement, wedding or anniversary, a house-warming or retirement, or giving a new look to Christmas.

With so many occasions to celebrate, it's not surprising that novelty cakes are becoming increasingly popular, and they can be a very rewarding way of expressing your own artistic skill. While the simplest designs can look most attractive, the more elaborate ones can truly be described as art forms in their own right!

Novelty cakes are easier to make than you might think, if you start off right. A well-made basic cake is an essential foundation for success, and you will find the recipes for the mixtures used in this book's cakes on pages 128-133. It's equally important to match the right icing to different types of cake, and you will find guidance on this, as well as recipes for various icings, on pages 134-7. Full instructions on the icing and decorating techniques which contribute so much to the finished appearance of a cake are given on pages 138-141.

Provided you start with some of the simpler designs, working up to more complicated ones as your skills increase, remember to practise a new design or technique on an upturned cake tin, plate or work surface rather than the cake itself to begin with, and above all allow yourself plenty of time, you will soon become proficient with novelty cakes.

EQUIPMENT

As with all cookery, the right equipment makes all the difference to the result. For success in novelty cake-making you will need:

Aspic cutters: tiny metal cutters, usually in playing card pip shapes, for cutting marzipan, fondant moulding paste into decorative shapes.

Biscuit cutters: larger versions of aspic cutters, available in greater assortment of shapes.

Bowls and basins: in assorted sizes; glass and china ones for mixing cake mixtures and icings, plastic ones (especially square containers with air-tight lids) for storing cakes, icings and decorations.

Cake boards: to present cakes.

Food colouring pens: for writing, adding decoration on cakes.

Greaseproof paper: to line cake tins, make icing bags.

Icing comb or scraper: to smooth sides of cake and make sharp corners. Serrated edge will give icing a wavy pattern.

Icing nozzles: metal nozzles in assorted sizes used for piping decorations on cakes.

Icing ruler: stainless steel or plastic, used to smooth icing surface.

Icing turntable: to swivel cake during icing.

Kitchen scissors: to cut paper and card.

Knives: to cut and shape cakes; must be sharp.

Liquid food colourings: colours for icings in liquid form; come in a good variety of shades.

Measuring spoons: complete set useful, in either metric or imperial measures.

Non-stick silicone paper: to line cake tins, or be base on which to make flat icing decorations.

Palette knives: large and small ones needed; used to spread icing.

Paste food colourings: colourings for icing, in paste rather than liquid form.

Pastry brush: to grease tins and lining paper and to apply glaze to cakes.

Rolling pin: to roll out marzipan and fondant moulding paste for cut-outs.

Sieves: nylon ones, to sift flour and icing sugar.

Spatulas: to scrape out cake mixtures and icings from bowls.

Skewers: wooden and metal ones; to test cakes, add colouring to icing, prick out patterns for icing decorations, and to hold cakes pieces to shape.

Tablespoons and teaspoons: for quick measuring.

Thin card: to make templates.

Tweezers: to position decorations on cakes.

Wire trays: for cooling cakes on.

Wooden cocktail sticks: to remove blobs and trails during decoration; to hold cake parts together.

Wooden spoons: to beat and mix.

CAKE TINS

When choosing cake tins, remember the best results come from good-quality, firm metal that conducts heat evenly and will not dent during storage.

Non-stick cake tins are available (follow manufacturers' instructions), otherwise tins must be greased and floured, or, most often, greased and lined. For greasing, use a light, taste-free oil, such as sunflower, or melted margarine. For lining, used greased greaseproof paper or non-stick silicone paper.

Sponge, sandwich and light fruit cake mixtures require base-lining only, though they are easier to remove from the tin if it is completely lined; Swiss roll and loaf tins should be single-lined on the base and sides; deep tins for rich fruit cakes should be double-lined.

To line a shallow rectangular tin

1 Cut a piece of greaseproof or non-stick silicone paper about 7.5 cm (3 inches) larger than the tin, and larger still if the tin sides are deeper than 2.5 cm (1 inch).
2 Place the tin on the paper and make a cut from the corner of the paper to each corner of the tin.
3 Grease inside the tin, then put in the paper so that it fits neatly, overlapping at the corners to give sharp angles. If using greaseproof, grease the paper again.

To line a loaf tin

Line the tin as described above, but cut the paper at least 15 cm (6 inches) larger than the tin.

To double line a deep tin

1 For a round tin, cut one or two strips of double greaseproof or non-stick silicone paper long enough to reach round the outside of the tin with enough to overlap, and wide enough to come 2.5 cm (1 inch) above the rim of the tin. Fold the bottom edge up about 2 cm (¾ inch) and crease it firmly. Open out and make slanting cuts into the folded strip at 2 cm (¾ inch) intervals.
2 Place the tin on a double thickness of greaseproof or non-stick silicone paper and draw round the base, then cut it out a little inside the line.
3 Grease the inside of the tin, place one paper circle in the base and grease just round the edge of the paper, if using greaseproof.
4 Place the long strips in the tin, pressing them against the sides with the cut edges spread over the base. Grease all over the side paper, if using greaseproof.
5 Position the second circle in the base of the tin and grease again if using greaseproof.
6 For a square tin, follow the instructions for a round tin above, but make folds into the corners of the long strips for the sides.

Measuring and cutting the lining paper for a shallow rectangular tin

Overlapping and folding the corner pieces of lining paper to give sharp angles

Preparing the side lining paper for a deep round cake tin

Fitting the lining paper, with the cut edge folded in over the base lining paper.

CAKE SHAPES

Although it is tempting to invest in some of the more exciting shaped cake tins, it is not necessary. Simple round and square cakes can easily be cut into a variety of interesting shapes.

Horseshoe

1 Using a paper pattern, cut out a central circle of about 5 cm (2 inches) from a 15-18 cm (6-7 inch) round cake; a 7.5-9 cm (3-3½ inch) circle for a 23-25 cm (9-10 inch) cake. Gradually enlarge the central circle as the size of the cake increases.

2 Cut out a wedge-shaped piece of cake to complete the horseshoe.

Using a template as guide when cutting a horseshoe-shaped cake. Although the knife is held at an angle as it cuts round the template, the blade is still carefully held upright in the cake to ensure a straight side.

Octagon

Cut the corners off a square cake as evenly as possible, to give eight sides all the same length. A template, simply made from a square of paper the size of the cake, makes cutting an octagonal shape from a round cake quite easy.

An octagon cut from a square cake   *An octagon cut from a round cake*

Hexagon

1 With a pair of compasses, measure the length from the centre of the cake to the edge. Make a mark on the edge.

2 Using the same measurement, position the compass point at the mark on the edge and make another mark with the other end, also on the edge.

3 Continue in this way marking off all round the edge of the cake, to give six equal sections.

4 Join the marks with straight lines and cut the cake downwards completely straight along the lines.

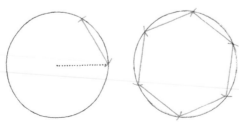

The steps in measuring the cuts for making a hexagon out of a round cake

Heart

1 Cut out a heart-shaped paper pattern, making the 'V' about 4 cm (1½ inches) deep on a 20 cm (8 inch) round cake and gradually deeper on larger cakes.

2 Place the pattern on the cake and cut out. The piece of cake taken out should be cut in half, reversed and placed at the other end of the cake, to make a point. Trim a small triangular piece off both sides to give a good fit. Join the cake pieces together with apricot glaze or butter cream.

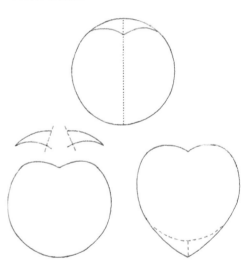

The steps in cutting a heart-shaped cake from a round one

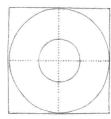

Pattern for cutting a nought from a round cake (and an eight from two round cakes)

Patterns for cutting numerals from square cakes: left, a four; below, a seven

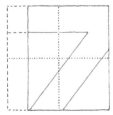

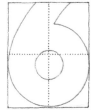

Patterns for cutting numerals from oblong cakes: below, a six; right, a two; below right, a five

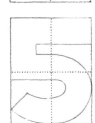

Shaping numeral cakes

Nought: bake a 23-30 cm/9-12 inch round cake. When cold cut a 7.5-12.5 cm/3-5 inch diameter hole in centre.

One: bake a 15 cm/6 inch square sandwich cake. Cut in half and position one piece above the other.

Two: bake a 29×21×4 cm/11½×8½×1½ inch slab cake or a 30×25×5 cm/12×10×2 inch cake. Cut a pattern, transfer to the cake and cut out.

Three: bake 2×20 cm/8 inch round sandwich cakes. Cut out a pattern, transfer to the cakes and cut out. Stick the two cakes together with jam or butter cream.

Four: bake an 18-25 cm/7-10 inch square sandwich cake. Cut out a pattern, transfer to the cake and cut out, taking care when removing the middle piece.

Five: bake a 29×21×4 cm/11½×8½×1½ inch slab cake or a 30×25×5 cm/12×10×2 inch cake. Cut a pattern, transfer to the cake and cut out.

Six or Nine: bake a 29×21×4 cm/11½×8½×1½ inch slab cake or a 30×25×5 cm/12×10×2 inch cake. Cut a pattern, transfer to the cake and cut out.

Seven: bake an 18-25 cm/7-10 inch square cake, or bake a 29×21×4 cm/11½×8½×1½ inch or a 30×25×5 cm/12×10×2 inch slab cake. Cut out a pattern, position on the cake and cut out.

Eight: bake 2×20 cm/8 inch round sandwich cakes. Cut out a pattern with a 7.5-9 cm/3-3½ inch circle out of the centre. Transfer to the cakes and cut out. Trim a piece off the side of each cake and sandwich together with jam or butter cream to make an eight.

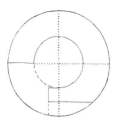

Left: patterns for cutting a three from two round cakes.

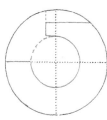

Right: the cake pieces cut and fitted together to form the numeral three.

CAKE MIXTURES

The following recipes will provide you with the basics for every type of novelty cake, from a simple cake for children to the most elaborate gâteau or special occasion rich fruit cake. In each case ingredient quantities and baking times are listed according to tin size.

Quick mix cake: beautifully easy to make, this is mixed and ready to bake in a matter of minutes by the all-in-one method. It should be used within a week of baking, and would be ideal for a child's birthday cake. It is specially easy to cut into shapes.

Madeira cake: made with butter, this has excellent keeping qualities and may be stored in an airtight container for 2-3 weeks, or in the freezer for 6 months. It has a firm texture, so may be covered with marzipan and royal icing like fruit cake (see pages 135-6), or glazed with

QUICK MIX CAKE

CAKE SIZES	2×18 cm (7 inch) sandwich tins	18 paper cake cases or patty tins	20 cm (8 inch) sandwich tin 20 cm (8 inch) ring mould 18 cm (7 inch) deep square tin	900 ml (½ pint) pudding basin*	about 26 paper cake case or patty tins	2×20 cm (8 inch) sandwich tins
soft (tub) margarine, chilled	100 g (4 oz)	100 g (4 oz)	100 g (4 oz)	100 g (4 oz)	175 g (6 oz)	175 g (6 oz)
caster sugar	100 g (4 oz)	100 g (4 oz)	100 g (4 oz)	100 g (4 oz)	175 g (6 oz)	175 g (6 oz)
eggs (size 1 or 2)	2	2	2	2	3	3
self-raising flour	100 g (4 oz)	100 g (4 oz)	100 g (4 oz)	100 g (4 oz)	175 g (6 oz)	175 g (6 oz)
baking powder	1 teaspoon	1 teaspoon	1 teaspoon	1 teaspoon	1½ teaspoons	1½ teaspoons
vanilla essence	4 drops	4 drops	4 drops	4 drops	6 drops	6 drops
approx cooking time	25-30 minutes	15-20 minutes	35-40 minutes	about 50 minutes	15-20 minutes	30-35 minutes

* add 25 g (1 oz) cornflower sifted with the flour

1 Put the margarine, sugar, eggs, sifted flour and baking powder and vanilla essence into a mixing bowl.
2 Mix with a wooden spoon or hand-held electric mixer until the ingredients are well combined, then beat for 1-2 minutes, until smooth and glossy.

3 Turn into a greased and single-lined tin (see page 125) and level the top. Bake in a preheated oven until well risen, just firm to the touch and beginning to shrink from the side of the tin.
4 Cool briefly in the tin, then turn on to a wire tray and leave to cool completely.

apricot jam and covered with fondant moulding paste (see page 137). It should be left for 24 hours after baking before icing. Madeira cake also cuts very well.
Rich fruit cake: ideal for weddings and traditional Christmas cake, this dark, moist fruit cake improves on keeping, so is ideal for making in advance. Ideally, it should be allowed to mature for 2-3 months, wrapped in greaseproof paper and foil, and stored in an airtight container, to be enjoyed at its best, but can be used perfectly well after only 2 weeks. It will keep for 6-8 months.

23 cm (9 inch) deep sandwich tin	2 oval ovenproof 600-700 ml (1-1¼ pint) glass dishes	28×18×4 cm (11×7×1½ inch) slab cake 20 cm (8 inch) round or petal tin 20 cm (8 inch) square tin	1 litre (2 pint) pudding basin*	29×21×4 cm (11½×8½× 1½ inch) slab cake	23 cm (9 inch) round or petal tin 23 cm (9 inch) square tin	30×25×5 cm (12×10×2 inch)slab cake
175 g (6 oz)	175 g (6 oz)	175 g (6 oz)	175 g (6 oz)	225 g (8 oz)	225 g (8 oz)	275 g (10 oz)
175 g (6 oz)	175 g (6 oz)	175 g (6 oz)	175 g (6 oz)	225 g (8 oz)	225 g (8 oz)	275 g (10 oz)
3	3	3	3	4	4	5
175 g (6 oz)	175 g (6 oz)	175 g (6 oz)	175 g (6 oz)	225 g (8 oz)	225 g (8 oz)	275 g (10 oz)
1½ teaspoons	1½ teaspoons	1½ teaspoons	1½ teaspoons	2 teaspoons	2 teaspoons	2½ teaspoons
6 drops	6 drops	6 drops	6 drops	8 drops	8 drops	10 drops
about 45 minutes	40-45 minutes	35-40 minutes	about 1 hour	about 40 minutes	about 1 hour	50-60 minutes

Other Flavours
Chocolate: omit the vanilla essence and add 1 tablespoon sifted cocoa powder for the 2-egg mixture; 1½ tablespoons for the 3-egg mixture; 2 tablespoons for the 4-egg mixture; and 2½ tablespoons for the 5-egg mixture.
Coffee: omit the vanilla essence and add 2 teaspoons instant coffee powder (not granules) or 1 tablespoon coffee essence for the 2-egg mixture; 1 tablespoon coffee powder or 1½ tablespoons coffee essence for the 3-egg mixture; 4 teaspoons coffee powder or 2 tablespoons coffee essence for the 4-egg mixture; and 5 teaspoons coffee powder or 2½ tablespoons coffee essence for the 5-egg mixture.
Orange or Lemon: omit the vanilla essence and add 2 teaspoons finely grated orange or lemon rind for the 2-egg mixture; 3 teaspoons for the 3-egg mixture; and so on.

MADEIRA CAKE

CAKE SIZES	15 cm (6 inch) round or square tin	18 cm (7 inch) round tin	18 cm (7 inch) round tin* 900 g (2 lb) loaf tin	18 cm (7 inch) square tin	20 cm (8 inch) round or petal shaped tin	20 cm (8 inch) round or petal shaped tin*
butter	100 g (4 oz)	100 g (4 oz)	150 g (6 oz)	150 g (6 oz)	150 g (6 oz)	200 g (8 oz)
caster sugar	100 g (4 oz)	100 g (4 oz)	150 g (6 oz)	150 g (6 oz)	150 g (6 oz)	200 g (8 oz)
self-raising flour	100 g (4 oz)	100 g (4 oz)	150 g (6 oz)	150 g (6 oz)	150 g (6 oz)	200 g (8 oz)
plain flour	50 g (2 oz)	50 g (2 oz)	75 g (3 oz)	75 g (3 oz)	75 g (3 oz)	100 g (4 oz)
eggs	2	2	3	3	3	4
grated lemon rind and juice	½-1 lemon	½-lemon	1 lemon	1 lemon	1 lemon	1½ lemons
approx cooking time	1 hour	50 minutes	1¼ hours	1 hour and 5-10 minutes	1 hour	1 hour and 15-20 minutes

* These quantities make a deeper cake

1 Grease and single-line the chosen tin (see page 125).
2 Cream the butter with the sugar until light, fluffy and very pale.
3 Sift the flours together. Beat the eggs into the creamed mixture, one at a time, following each addition with a spoonful of sifted flour.
4 Fold in the remaining flour, followed by the grated lemon rind and juice.
5 Bake in a preheated oven (see individual recipes for temperature and time) until well-risen, firm to the touch and golden-brown.
6 Cool in the tin for 5-10 minutes, then turn on to a wire tray and leave until cold. Do not peel off the lining paper but wrap the cake as it is in foil or store in an airtight container until required. Madeira cake may be frozen for up to

six months. Thaw completely, still in its wrapping, at room temperature before use.

Some flavour variations:
Orange Madeira: use orange juice and rind instead of lemon.
Ginger: omit the lemon rind and add 1 teaspoon ground ginger to the 2-egg mixture plus 2 pieces finely chopped stem ginger, if liked. Add 1½ teaspoons ground ginger to the 3-egg mixture; and 2 teaspoons to the 4-egg mixture with more chopped stem ginger as desired.
Coffee Walnut: omit the lemon rind and replace the lemon juice with coffee essence. Add 40 g (1½ oz) finely chopped walnuts to the 2-egg mixture; 50 g (2 oz) walnuts to the 3-egg mixture; and 65 g (2½ oz) walnuts to the 4-egg mixture.

20 cm (8 inch) square tin	23 cm (9 inch) round tin	28×18×4 cm (11×7×1½ inch) slab cake	23 cm (9 inch) round or petal shaped tin*	23 cm (9 inch) square tin	25 cm (10 inch) round or petal shaped tin	30×25×5 cm (12×10×2 inch) slab cake
200 g (8 oz)	200 g (8 oz)	200 g (8 oz)	250 g (10 oz)	250 g (10 oz)	250 g (10 oz)	250 g (10 oz)
200 g (8 oz)	200 g (8 oz)	200 g (8 oz)	250 g (10 oz)	250 g (10 oz)	250 g (10 oz)	250 g (10 oz)
200 g (8 oz)	200 g (8 oz)	200 g (8 oz)	250 g (10 oz)	250 g (10 oz)	250 g (10 oz)	250 g (10 oz)
100 g (4 oz)	100 g (4 oz)	100 g (4 oz)	125 g (5 oz)	125 g (5 oz)	125 g (5 oz)	125 g (5 oz)
4	4	4	5	5	5	5
1½ lemons	1½ lemons	1½ lemons	2 lemons	2 lemons	2 lemons	2 lemons
1 hour and 15-20 mintes	1 hour and 10 minutes	1-1¼ hours	1 hour and 30-40 minutes	1 hour and 25-30 minutes	1 hour and 20 minutes	1 hour and 15-20 minutes

RICH FRUIT CAKE INGREDIENTS

SQUARE	13 cm (5 inch)	15 cm (6 inch)	18 cm (7 inch)	20 cm (8 inch)	23 cm (9 inch)	25 cm (10 inch)	28 cm (11 inch)	30 cm (12 inch)
ROUND or PETAL SHAPED	15 cm (6 inch)	18 cm (7 inch)	20 cm (8 inch)	23 cm (9 inch)	25 cm (10 inch)	28 cm (11 inch)	30 cm (12 inch)	
SLAB CAKE				29×21×4 cm (11½×8½× 1½ inch)	30×25×5 cm (12×10× 2 inch)			
currants	150 g (5 oz)	225 g (8 oz)	350 g (12 oz)	450 g (1 lb)	625 g (1 lb 6 oz)	775 g (1 lb 12 oz)	1.2 kg (2 lb 8 oz)	1.4 kg (3 lb)
sultanas	50 g (2 oz)	90 g (3½ oz)	125 g (4½ oz)	200 g (7 oz)	225 g (8 oz)	375 g (13 oz)	400 g (14 oz)	500 g (1 lb 2 oz)
raisins	50 g (2 oz)	90 g (3½ oz)	125 g (4½ oz)	200 g (7 oz)	225 g (8 oz)	375 g (13 oz)	400 g (14 oz)	500 g (1 lb 2 oz)
glacé cherries	40 g (1½ oz)	65 g (2½ oz)	75 g (3 oz)	100 g (4 oz)	150 g (5 oz)	225 g (8 oz)	300 g (10 oz)	350 g (12 oz)
mixed peel, chopped	25 g (1 oz)	50 g (2 oz)	50 g (2 oz)	75 g (3 oz)	100 g (4 oz)	150 g (5 oz)	200 g (7 oz)	250 g (9 oz)
blanched almonds, chopped	25 g (1 oz)	50 g (2 oz)	50 g (2 oz)	75 g (3 oz)	100 g (4 oz)	150 g (5 oz)	200 g (7 oz)	250 g (9 oz)
lemon rind, grated	¼ lemon	½ lemon	¾ lemon	1 lemon	1 lemon	1 lemon	1½ lemons	2 lemons
plain flour	100 g (3½ oz)	175 g (6 oz)	200 g (7½ oz)	350 g (12 oz)	400 g (14 oz)	600 g (1 lb 5 oz)	700 g (1 lb 8 oz)	825 g (1 lb 13 oz)
ground cinnamon	½ teaspoon	½ teaspoon	¾ teaspoon	1 teaspoon	1½ teaspoons	2 teaspoons	2½ teaspons	2¾ teaspoons
ground mixed spice	¼ teaspoon	¼ teaspoon	½ teaspoon	¾ teaspoon	1 teaspoon	1¼ teaspoons	1½ teaspoons	1¾ teaspoons
butter	75 g (3 oz)	150 g (5 oz)	175 g (6 oz)	275 g (10 oz)	350 g (12 oz)	500 g (1 lb 2 oz)	600 g (1 lb 5 oz)	800 g (1 lb 12 oz)

SQUARE	13 cm (5 inch)	15 cm (6 inch)	18 cm (7 inch)	20 cm (8 inch)	23 cm (9 inch)	25 cm (10 inch)	28 cm (11 inch)	30 cm (12 inch)
ROUND or PETAL SHAPED	15 cm (6 inch)	18 cm (7 inch)	20 cm (8 inch)	23 cm (9 inch)	25 cm (10 inch)	28 cm (11 inch)	30 cm (12 inch)	
SLAB CAKE				29×21×4 cm (11½×8½× 1½ inch)	30×25×5 cm (12×10× 2 inch)			
soft brown sugar	75 g (3 oz)	150 g (5 oz)	175 g (6 oz)	275 g (10 oz)	350 g (12 oz)	500 g (1 lb 2 oz)	600 g (1 lb 5 oz)	800 g (1 lb 12 oz)
eggs (size 2)	1½	2½	3	5	6	9	11	14
black treacle (optional)	1 teaspoon	1 teaspoon	1 tablespoon	1 tablespoon	1 tablespoon	2 tablespoons	2 tablespoons	2 tablespoons
approx cooking time	2 hours	2½ hours	2¾ hours	3¼ hours	3¾ hours	4¼-4½ hours	5¼-5½ hours	6-6½ hours
approx cooked weight	750 g (1½ lb)	1.25 kg (2½ lb)	1.5 kg (3¼ lb)	2 kg (4½ lb)	2.75 kg (6 lb)	4 kg (9 lb)	5 kg (11 lb)	6.5 kg (14 lb)
brandy, added after cooking	2 tablespoons	3 tablespoons	3 tablespoons	4 tablespoons	5 tablespoons	6 tablespoons	7 tablespoons	8 tablespoons

1 Grease and double-line the chosen cake tin (see page 125).
2 Mix together the currants, sultanas and raisins in a bowl.
3 Quarter the glacé cherries, rinse under warm water and pat dry. Add to the dried fruit mixture together with the mixed peel, almonds and grated lemon rind. Mix well.
4 Sift the flour with the cinnamon and mixed spice.
5 Cream the butter until soft, then add the sugar until light, fluffy and much paler in colour.
6 Add the eggs to the creamed mixture one at a time, following each addition with a spoonful of spiced flour and beating the mixture thoroughly.
7 Fold in the remaining flour, followed by the dried fruit mixture.
8 Add the black treacle, if used.
9 Turn into the prepared tin and level the top. Using the back of a spoon, make a slight hollow in the centre of the mixture, so that the cake will have a flat surface when baked.
10 Fold sheets of brown paper into strips of 6 thicknesses, to measure the circumference and depth of the tin. Tie around the tin to protect the cake from forming a thick, tough outside edge during cooking.
11 Bake in a preheated oven until a skewer inserted into the centre comes out clean. If the cake shows signs of overbrowning during baking, lay a sheet of greaseproof paper lightly over the top.
12 Leave to cool in the tin, then turn on to a wire tray. Leave to cool completely.
13 Prick the top of the cake all over with a skewer, then spoon several tablespoons of brandy over the top. Wrap the cake in greaseproof paper and foil and store in an airtight container. Pour brandy over the pricked surface every two weeks during storing.

ICINGS AND GLAZES

Icing for novelty cakes needs to be firm – soft glacé icing is not very suitable – and should provide a smooth surface for decoration: flat-iced cakes are best, rather than those with a peaked finish, as with rough Royal icing or American frosting.

Royal icing (see page 134) is ideal for fruit cakes, but may also be used to cover Madeira cake (see pages 130-1). It must always be applied over a layer of marzipan, which makes a smooth surface on the cake and, therefore, gives the icing a smooth surface, too.

Royal icing can be made in any quantity as long as you allow 1 egg white to each 225 g (8 oz) icing sugar. It is better to make up not more than 900 g (2 lb) at a time because the icing keeps better in small quantities.

Royal icing sets very firm, though the addition of glycerine (available from chemists) helps soften it and makes cutting easier. It should be beaten with a wooden spoon rather than an electric mixer, which creates too many air-bubbles. It is best applied in two coats, and each coat should be left to dry for at least 24 hours. The icing can be stored in an airtight container in a cool place for about 2 days and must be stirred very thoroughly before use.

In its natural state, Royal icing is a dazzling white, but may, of course, be coloured in any shade using either liquid or paste food colourings (see page 139). It is ideal for piping, as it holds its shape so well, and makes very successful decorations, either thickened with extra icing sugar, or thinned down with a few drops of lemon juice for flooding run-outs (see pages 140-1).

Marzipan (see page 136), also called Almond Paste, is not only rolled out and used to cover cakes before Royal icing or Fondant moulding paste is applied. It can also be tinted with food colouring and used to make moulded cake decorations, such as flowers and fruits, or rolled out to make flat cut-outs, such as leaves, stars or horseshoes. To colour marzipan, simply add several drops of the chosen colour or colours, then knead and squeeze the marzipan until the colour is distributed evenly throughout with no streaking. Paste colour may be used in the same way. If the marzipan becomes a little soft, knead in a little sifted icing sugar as well. Marzipan is easily made, but may also be bought from supermarkets and speciality shops.

Fondant moulding paste (see page 137) is a particularly good covering for novelty cakes, as it is so pliable and can be moulded easily to any shape. It is also very simple to make (liquid glucose or glucose syrup is available from chemists), though it is easiest to make up quantities of up to 900 g (2 lb) only, because of the kneading that is required. A 450-700 g (1-1½ lb) quantity is ideal; ready-made Fondant moulding paste is available from large supermarkets and specialised shops and suppliers, both in small amounts and in bulk, which may be more convenient.

Butter cream (see page 137) is a particularly versatile icing, which also has the advantages of being very easy to make, and of freezing well. It can be applied directly to a cake, or over a layer of marzipan. It can be coloured and flavoured in all sorts of ways, it spreads easily and pipes well. It can be used to decorate cakes covered with Fondant

moulding paste, as well as those iced with butter cream.

Here are some flavour variations on the basic recipe on page 137:
Coffee butter cream: omit the vanilla and replace 1 tablespoon of the milk with coffee essence or very strong black coffee; or beat in 2-3 teaspoons coffee powder with the icing sugar.
Chocolate butter cream: add 25-40 g (1-1½ oz) melted plain chocolate; or dissolve 1-2 tablespoons sifted cocoa powder in a little hot water to give a thin paste, cool and beat into the icing in place of some of the milk.
Orange or Lemon butter cream: omit the vanilla, replace the milk with orange or lemon juice and add the finely grated rind of 1 orange or lemon and a little orange or yellow liquid food colouring.
Mocha butter cream: dissolve 1-2 teaspoons cocoa powder in 1 tablespoon coffee essence or very strong black coffee and add in place of some or all the milk.
Almond butter cream: replace the vanilla with almond essence and beat in about 2 tablespoons very finely chopped toasted almonds if liked. A few drops of green colouring may be added to give a pale almond green coloured icing.
Apricot butter cream: omit the vanilla and milk and beat in 3 tablespoons sieved apricot jam, a pinch of grated lemon rind, a squeeze of lemon juice and a touch of orange liquid food colouring.

ROYAL ICING

MAKES 675 g (1½ lb)
Enough to ice a 20 cm (8 inch) round
cake

3 egg whites
675 g (1½ lb) icing sugar, sifted
3 teaspoons lemon juice, strained
1-1½ teaspoons glycerine (optional)

1 Put the egg whites into a clean bowl and
beat until frothy. Using a wooden spoon,
gradually beat in half the icing sugar.
2 Add the lemon juice, glycerine if used,
and the remaining sugar a tablespoon or so
at a time. Beat well until the mixture is
smooth, very white and stands in soft
peaks.
3 Transfer the icing to a sealed airtight
container or cover the bowl with a damp
cloth to prevent a skin forming and leave
to stand for an hour or so, to allow the air
bubbles in the icing to disperse.
4 The icing is now ready to be used for
coating a cake, or it can be thickened a
little with extra sifted icing sugar to pipe
stars, flowers and other decorations; or it
can be thinned a little by adding a little
lightly beaten egg white or lemon juice
and used to flood run-outs.

To flat-ice a cake ready for decoration
1 Attach the cake to a cake board 2.5-5 cm
(1-2 inches) larger than the cake with a dab
of icing, or place on an icing turntable. Put
a quantity of icing on top of the cake and
smooth out with a palette knife, using a
paddling movement to dispel any remaining air bubbles and spread the icing out
evenly.
2 Draw an icing ruler evenly across the
top of the cake, holding it an angle of
about **30°** and without exerting additional
pressure.
3 Remove surplus icing by running a
palette knife round the top edge of the

Using an icing ruler to smooth the royal icing on top
of the cake.

Removing surplus icing by running a palette knife
round the top edge of the cake.

Using an icing comb to smooth the icing on the side of
the cake

The completed smooth and flat icing, ready to receive
decorations.

cake, holding it at right angles to the cake.
Leave to dry.
4 Spread a thin covering layer of icing
round the sides of the cake, again using a
paddling movement.
5 Hold an icing comb or scraper at an
angle of about 45° to the cake. Swivelling
the cake on the turntable if used, or using
your free hand to rotate it slowly, move
the comb slowly and evenly round the
sides of the cake. Remove the comb at an
angle and fairly quickly, so the join is
hardly noticeable.
6 Remove any excess icing from the top
of the cake with a palette knife, again
rotating the cake. Leave to dry.

MARZIPAN

MAKES 450 g (1 lb)
100 g (4 oz) caster sugar
100g (4 oz) icing sugar, sifted
225 g (8 oz) ground almonds
1 teaspoon lemon juice
few drops of almond essence
1 egg or 2 egg yolks

1 Combine the sugars and ground almonds in a mixing bowl and make a well in the centre.
2 Add the lemon juice, almond essence and sufficient egg or egg yolk to mix to a firm but manageable dough.
3 Turn on to a board or work surface dusted with a little icing sugar and knead until smooth. Do not over-knead or the marzipan will be oily. If not using immediately, wrap in foil or clingfilm and store for 2-3 days.

APRICOT GLAZE

175 g (6 oz) apricot jam
2 tablespoons water

1 Put the jam and water into a small saucepan and heat gently until the jam has melted, stirring occasionally.
2 Pass through a sieve into a clean pan.
3 Return to the boil, then simmer until fairly thick but not stiff. Allow to cool. If not using immediately, store in an airtight container in the refrigerator for up to 1 week, then boil and cool again before using.

Covering a cake with marzipan

1 Place almost half the marzipan on a work surface dredged with icing sugar, or between 2 sheets of clingfilm. Roll out evenly until 2.5cm (1 inch) larger than the top of the cake.
2 Brush cake top with apricot glaze.

Inverting the cake on to the rolled-out marzipan. A layer of icing sugar or clingfilm under the marzipan should ensure that cake and marzipan can now be easily turned right way up without sticking to the work surface.

Unrolling the marzipan strip cut to fit the side of the cake.

Shaping the marzipan round the top edge of the cake.

Smoothing out the joins in the marzipan.

3 Invert cake on to marzipan (first removing the top layer of clingfilm, if used, from the marzipan) and carefully turn the cake right way up. Now remove remaining clingfilm from marzipan, if used, or brush off any excess icing sugar. Trim off excess marzipan and smooth edge with small palette kife.
4 Stand cake, marzipan side up, on a cake board and brush sides with apricot glaze.
5 Cut 2 pieces of string, one measuring the depth of the cake, the other measuring the circumference. Roll out

the remaining marzipan and, using the string as a guide, cut a strip measuring the depth and circumference of the cake.
6 Loosely roll the marzipan strip into a coil. Place one end on the side of the cake and unroll carefully, moulding the marzipan to the side of the cake as you go, and making sure the marzipan touches the board. Smooth the join with a palette knife.
7 Store the cake, uncovered, for 4-6 days before icing, if a fruit cake; or for 24-48 hours if a Madeira cake.

FONDANT MOULDING PASTE

MAKES 450 g (1 lb)

450 g (1 lb) icing sugar
1 egg white
50 g (2 oz) liquid glucose or glucose syrup
liquid or paste food colouring (optional)

1 Sift the icing sugar into a bowl and make a well in the centre.
2 Add the egg white and liquid glucose. Beat with a wooden spoon, gradually drawing in the icing sugar from the side of the bowl, until the mixture is stiff.
3 Dip your hands into a mixture of icing sugar and cornflour, then knead the icing in the bowl, using the fingertips and kneading in a circular movement. Add food colouring sparingly, if used, and knead again until smooth and evenly coloured.
4 If not using immediately, store in a tightly sealed airtight container or sealed thick polythene bag for 2-3 days in a cool place.

To cover a cake with fondant moulding paste

1 If the cake is covered with marzipan, brush lightly all over with egg white or leave it as it is. If the cake is uncovered, brush all over with apricot glaze (see page 136).
2 On a sheet of clingfilm or non-stick silicone paper on a work surface and dredged lightly with a mixture of cornflour and icing sugar, roll out the fondant until 13-15 cm (5-6 inches) larger than the cake.
3 Support the icing on a rolling pin, drawing off the clingfilm if used, and position the icing centrally on top of the cake.
4 Dip your fingertips in a mixture of icing sugar and cornflour and press the icing over the sides of the cake, working from the centre to the edge, then down the sides, in a circular movement. Trim any excess icing from the base.
5 Leave for at least 24 hours and preferably 2-3 days to dry completely before decorating.

BUTTER CREAM ICING

Makes enough to cover the top and sides of an 18 cm (7 inch) cake, or to fill and cover the top. For flavour and colour variations see page 134.

100 g (4 oz) butter or soft margarine
175-225 g (6-8 oz) icing sugar, sifted
few drops of vanilla essence
1-2 tablespoons milk

1 Cream the butter or margarine until very soft.
2 Gradually beat in enough sugar and milk to give a fairly firm but spreading cosistency. Beat in the vanilla.
3 If not using immediately, store in a sealed airtight container for up to 1 week in the refrigerator.

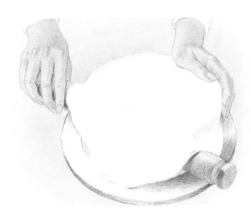

Using a rolling pin to place the rolled-out fondant moulding paste over the top of the cake.

Pressing the fondant moulding paste down round the sides of the cake.

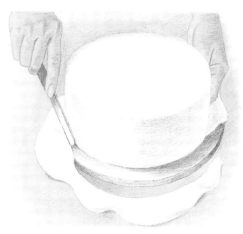

Using a sharp knife to trim off excess fondant moulding paste.

ICING TECHNIQUES

Icing bag

When piping icing it is easier to control the flow if you use an icing bag rather than a icing pump, which consists of a tube and plunger. Nylon icing bags can be bought in varying sizes, but it is easy, and cheaper, to make your own icing bags from greaseproof paper. Make up several different sizes at one time.

Making a paper icing bag

1 Cut a piece of greaseproof paper to a square: 25 cm (10 inches) makes a useful sized bag. Fold in half to form a triangle.
2 Fold triangle in half to make smaller triangle (A to B) and press folds firmly.
3 Open out smaller triangle and fold bottom half of triangle (B) up to folded line (C), creasing firmly.
4 Continue to fold bag over (D to F) and then C to A, creasing firmly.
5 Secure join (A to E) with sellotape or fold top point (A) over twice to secure. Cut 1 cm (½ inch) off tip of bag and open out to insert nozzle.

Using an icing bag

Insert the nozzle into the tip of the bag. Half to two-thirds fill the bag with icing, pushing it down well towards the tip with a small palette knife or teaspoon. Fold the top over carefully. Hold the bag as illustrated, and apply steady pressure until icing comes out of nozzle.

Place paper icing bag across palm with nozzle towards fingertips. Place thumb on folded end of bag, then fold over other four fingers to hold bag tightly. Use other hand to hold bag steady and apply pressure.

With a nylon icing bag, place thumb and forefinger round icing in bag and twist bag tightly two or three times. Hold bag over twist and apply pressure

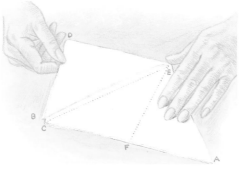

Folding bottom of triangle (B) to (C).

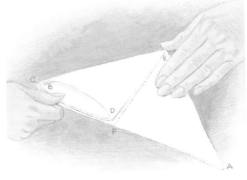

Continuing to fold bag (D) to (F).

Securing join.

Folding the end of a paper icing bag.

with other hand.

For fine work and lattice, hold bag in both hands with thumbs over end, using rest of hands to support the weight of the bag underneath.

Icing nozzles

These are also known as pipes and tubes. A large range of different makes is available, falling into two main types: plain-based, which are ideal for use in paper icing bags, and screw-on, which need a connector when used with a nylon icing bag.

Icing nozzles are sold by number,

which can be confusing as the numbering is not universally standardized. Always check individual manufacturers' charts when buying. Check, too, that nozzles are perfectly shaped, with no dents or defective seams.

Icing nozzles come in a great variety of sizes. The two basic shapes are plain and star. Plain nozzles are used for writing, for outlining run-outs (see page 140) and for piping lines, dots, lattice and lacework. Star nozzles vary widely in size and shape of star produced, ranging from 5 to 10 points in the star, and can be used to make many designs. Other useful nozzle shapes are the shell, for edging and borders, and the petal, for piping floral decorations (see page 140).

Using icing nozzles

All the following techniques are easily acquired with practice. Practise on paper, a plate or upturned cake tin before piping the icing on to the cake surface. Remove any blobs or trails of icing with a cocktail stick. Always leave piped icing to dry completely before overpiping.

Straight lines: place the tip of the nozzle where the line is to begin, and as the icing emerges from the bag, lift the nozzle about 2.5 cm (1 inch) above the surface. Move your hand in the direction you want to take the line, using the other hand to steady the bag and keep the icing emerging steadily. Just before where the line should end, lower the tip of the nozzle to the surface and break it off evenly with a rapid movement.

Curved lines: prick out the curve with a fine skewer before proceeding as above.

Lattice: pipe a series of straight lines in one direction, keeping them evenly spaced. Leave to dry, then turn cake and pipe a second series of parallel lines over the first, at right angles for squares, or at 45 for diamonds.

Dots: hold a plain nozzle upright with the tip just touching the surface. Squeeze bag gently, at the same time lifting the nozzle, until the size of the dot required is achieved. Remove the nozzle quickly with a slight down and up movement.

Writing: for block letterings, first prick out the design on to the cake, then follow the pattern, using a plain nozzle. For freehand writing, write out the words on a piece of paper first, to see how much room will be needed.

Stars: hold a star nozzle upright just above the surface of the cake. Pipe out the size of star required, then quickly lift off with a down and up movement.

Rosettes: pipe as for stars, but using a circular movement.

Shells: hold a shell or star nozzle at an angle to the surface and a little above it. Start in the centre of the shell and first move the nozzle away from you, keeping an even pressure of icing, then back towards you, exerting a little more

Icing nozzles, top: small, medium and large stars; bottom: small and large shells

pressure to form the 'fat' part of the shell. Release pressure to allow icing to tail off and pull off sharply to make a point.

Colouring icing

Liquid food colourings are available in every shade: they should be used with caution, to give a subtle, not garish effect. The best way to tint icing is to dip a skewer into the bottle of liquid colouring and add a few drops at a time to the icing, or add a minute amount of paste colouring.

Holding a paper icing bag.

An alternative way of holding a nylon bag for fine piping work.

Holding a nylon icing bag.

DECORATIONS IN ICING

Royal icing is used for piping flowers and leaves of all types and for run-outs. All icing decorations should be made well in advance (2-3 days and up to 3-4 weeks), and allowed to dry out completely. Store in an airtight container.

See the following pages for making moulded flowers: page 40, dandelion; page 74, hyacinth; page 84, water lily; page 92, fuschia; page 94, polyanthus; page 96, orchid; page 106, Christmas rose.

ICING FLOWERS

To pipe flowers, you need an icing nail, non-stick silicone paper cut into 2.5-5 cm (1-2 inch) squares, and an icing bag fitted with a large, medium or fine petal nozzle. A medium nozzle can be used for most flowers. Half fill the bag with icing and fold down. Secure a square of paper to the icing nail.

Rose

Hold the piping bag with the thin edge of the nozzle upwards. Squeezing evenly and twisting the nail at the same time, pipe a tight coil for the centre of the rose. Add five or six petals, one at a time, piping and twisting at the same time, but taking each petal only three-quarters of the way round the flower.

Using an icing nail to pipe rose flowers

Begin in a different part of the flower each time, and keep the base of the nozzle in towards the centre of the flower, so that it keeps its shape.

Daisy

Pipe five or six pointed but slightly rounded separate petals. Using a medium plain nozzle, pipe a large dot in the centre of the flower, using a contrasting colour.

Narcissus

Begin with the thick edge of the petal

nozzle to the centre. Keep the nozzle flat and work each petal separately. Gently squeeze out the icing and take the tip outwards to a point, keeping it flat, then bring it back towards the centre, twisting it slightly and gradually releasing the pressure; break off. Make five more petals in the same way, starting by placing the nozzle just under the previous petal, so that each petal slightly underlaps its neighbour. Leave to dry, then add the centre using a small petal nozzle and yellow icing. Pipe a cup in the centre, making a complete circle of icing while rotating the nail. Leave to dry, then pipe dots of orange icing in the centre of the cup for the stamens.

Primrose

This is made in a similar way to a narcissus but has five almost heart-shaped petals. When the petal nozzle is out from the centre, instead of bringing it straight back, dip it towards the centre and then take it out again before returning completely to the centre. This will give a heart shape. Make four more petals in the same way, making them underlap slightly, then leave to dry. Pipe a few tiny dots in the centre, using a fine plain nozzle and deep yellow or pale orange icing.

ICING RUN-OUTS

The run-outs technique can be used to make all kinds of shapes. The chosen shape is first outlined with piping, then filled in and flooded with softer icing. Run-outs can be piped straight on to the cake or on to non-stick silicone paper and attached to the cake with icing when dry. As they are very fragile, it is a good idea to make spares.

To make run-outs to attach to the cake, first draw the outline on a piece of card. Lay non-stick silicone paper over the drawing, attaching firmly. Using a fine plain nozzle, trace round the outline. Leave to dry. Thin the icing with a little lemon juice or lightly beaten egg white until it just flows. For larger shapes, spoon the icing into the centre of the outline and let it flow out to fill the outline, using a skewer to guide it. For smaller shapes, pipe the flowing icing into the outline until filled, using a paper icing bag without a nozzle. Prick any air bubbles which appear with a pin and leave to dry for 2-3 days.

ANIMALS

Use 40-50 g (1½-2 oz) of Fondant moulding paste or white marzipan for each animal. As well as the animals here, see page 24 for teddy bears.

Rabbit

Colour all but a minute piece of the fondant pink, grey or brown. Shape ⅔ into the body of an upstanding rabbit then the remainder into two long ears, four feet and a head with a slightly pointed nose. Stick the head to the body with water; then attach the ears and feet. Use the tiny piece of white icing to make a tail. Mark the eyes and nose with a skewer or cocktail stick.

Dog

Colour the fondant a suitable colour and use ⅞ of it to make a cylinder. Shape this into a body with fairly short legs with small feet; then form a short tail, attaching it and curling it slightly over the dog's back.

Cat

Colour the fondant any cat colour you like. Mould ⅔ into a long cylinder and fold under about ⅓ for the back legs, split the other end in half and shape for the front paws. Shape a ball for the head with two ears and a nose. Attach the head to the body and fold one of the front paws over the other. Make a tail and attach. Mark eyes and nose with a skewer and then paint in with brown food colouring; paint toes on the paws.

Frog

Colour the icing a deep green. Reserve ⅓ and shape the remainder into a frog's body with one end thicker and bigger than the other. Make a cut into the thicker end of the body and shape the head so it is slightly upwards. Halve the lower piece for two legs and feet. Press

the body so it has a large head. Use the remaining icing to make back legs. Attach to the body. Mark the eyes and mouth and paint on spots, toes and eyes with a darker green food colouring.

Lamb

Colour the fondant a creamy colour and use to shape into a cylinder with a lump at one end. Shape the lump into a head with ears and then mould out 4 small legs from under the cylinder and a tiny tail from the other end. 'Rough up' the icing with a cocktail stick to resemble wool, leaving the legs and head smooth. Mark in the eyes and then paint the face and legs with black or dark brown liquid food colouring.

Mouse

Mice can be pink white, brown, black or grey. Remove a small piece and roll into a tail. Mould the remainder into a body with a small piece at one end from the head, with 2 ears and a pointed nose. Make the body so it is fairly rounded with two marked back legs and two tiny front feet. Attach the tail and mark in eyes, nose and mouth.

Tortoise

Colour 20 g (¾ oz) fondant a pale green and the remainder a greenish-brown. Shape the larger piece into a body shell, flat underneath and the edges slightly turning up. Make a notch at the front for the head and four small notches at the sides for legs. Shape half the green icing into a head and attach at the front, and then the remainder into four feet, attaching these at the appropriate places. Mark in eyes, nose, and mouth and toes with a skewer and a series of irregular touching circles on the shell with circular shapes inside each.

INDEX

ACKNOWLEDGEMENTS

Photographer
MICHAEL MICHAELS

Photographic styling
MARIA JACQUES

Preparation of food for photography
ROSEMARY WADEY

Illustrations
ANGELA BARNES

Step by step illustrations
PATRICIA CAPON

Cover Photograph
VERNON MORGAN

Preparation of food for cover photograph
ROSEMARY WADEY